*The ponies of Shetland are the smallest and probably the purest of the British breeds.*

# LEADING THE FIELD

*British Native Breeds of Horses and Ponies*

Elwyn Hartley Edwards

*Photographs by Kit Houghton*

STANLEY PAUL

London   Sydney   Auckland   Johannesburg

Stanley Paul & Co. Ltd

An imprint of the Random Century Group
20 Vauxhall Bridge Road, London SW1V 2SA

Random Century Australia (Pty) Ltd
20 Alfred Street, Milsons Point, Sydney, NSW 2061

Random Century New Zealand Ltd
191 Archers Road, PO Box 40-086, Auckland 10

Century Hutchinson South Africa (Pty) Ltd
PO Box 337, Bergvlei 2012, South Africa

First published 1992

Typeset in Sabon by SX Composing Ltd, Rayleigh, Essex
Printed and bound in Singapore by
Tien Wah Press (PTE) Ltd

A catalogue record for this book is available
upon request from the British Library

ISBN 0-09-175332-5

# Contents

# Acknowledgements

The author wishes to express his thanks to John Abbot who typed, collated and processed the text.

The author and publishers are grateful to the following for permission to reproduce archive material: Arthur Ackermann & Son Ltd, page 136; the Stewards of the Jockey Club, page 140; Christie, Manson and Woods Ltd, page 145.

# Foreword

In terms of quantity the British horse product has never approached that of other and larger European nations, many of whose horse-breeding industries have benefited from active state support over a long period. Traditionally, British governments have obstinately refused to give practical recognition to a horse-breeding industry outside that of the Thoroughbred racehorse. As a result, what industry exists relies upon a fragmented private enterprise carried on by individual enthusiasts who are divided between no less than 46 different and autonomous breed societies. As yet, there is no single unifying umbrella organisation to co-ordinate their efforts, and when it comes to assessing the market target, breeding objectively to that end and then promoting the product vigorously and effectively, the British enterprise cannot compare with the organised, well-financed and market-conscious industries of mainland Europe.

That is the debit side of the balance sheet and will need now to be addressed with some urgency. Following the example of their fellow Europeans, British breeders are, indeed, becoming increasingly aware that breeding is no longer a matter of 'the best to the best and hope for the best'. More and more of them appreciate that proposed matings must include a study of the genetic background, covering not only pedigrees but the all-important performance records of both partners as well as those of their progeny.

Despite the admitted disadvantages of the British system there are, nonetheless, significant and encouraging factors to act as a counter-balance.

Largely because of its insularity Britain has a unique equine heritage of inestimable value and great genetic variety. The British climate may be the despair of overseas visitors, but together with the country's particular soil structures it is ideally suited to the raising of equine stock.

British breeders, too, are innately skilful and practise high standards of management. Furthermore, they have access to a very wide choice of Thoroughbred blood, the greatest single factor in equine development over the last 250 years; they make more general use of it than most, and are naturally experienced in the management of this necessarily high-couraged super-horse.

As a distinctive encouragement to breeding and development that also provides useful guide-lines to the market requirement, there is the extraordinarily high participation in a wide variety of horse sports. There are, indeed, more riders in Britain, *per capita* of the total population, than anywhere else, and the opportunities for competition are correspondingly numerous.

Finally, there are the nine native breeds of British ponies, renowned for their extreme soundness, stamina and hardiness, and for their good sense and courage, as well as those relatively more recently established breeds, all of which are discussed in this book. The ponies are valuable in their own right and also because of their potential to provide first and second crosses to the Thoroughbred.

The background to the development of all the breeds is examined in some detail, in what is a deliberate attempt to put the horses and ponies in perspective within the fascinating jigsaw of equine development.

If the book goes a little way towards encouraging a realisation of the values of the British equine heritage it will have served its purpose and my indulgence in national chauvinism may, perhaps, be forgiven.

EHE
Chwilog 1991

# Introduction

In relation to the size of Britain and Ireland, the horse and pony population is disproportionately rich and remarkably varied. Its contribution to the equine population of the world is equally great: indeed, the nine breeds of native or indigenous ponies that have evolved there since the after-effects of the Ice Age separated Britain from Europe, some 20-10,000 years ago, are a unique distillation of the pony types of the Western world. They are thus of incomparable value far beyond their native shores, both in their own right and as the basis for future development.

The horse breeds, as distinct from the ponies, were established in Britain much later and cannot be termed indigenous, but they too have a significant influence. Of the heavy horses, the massive, majestically moving Shire, descendant of the English Great Horse, is a product of the sixteenth century, along with the older-established Suffolk Punch, whilst the last of the British heavy horse trio, the Clydesdale, has developed over no more than the past 150 years, but has lost no time in creating a sizeable presence in both North America and Australia.

The lighter-built Irish Draught, like its heavier cousins, owes much to the Flemish and northern French horses brought into Britain and Ireland after the Conquest. That other important British breed, the Cleveland Bay, although its ancestors were about in mediaeval times, was heavily influenced by the Spanish horses and possibly the North African Barbs that were imported into the north-east of Britain in the latter part of the seventeenth century.

As for the Thoroughbred, the world's super-horse, that is an all-British 'invention'. It evolved in seventeenth- and eighteenth-century England as a result of crossing Oriental (Arab) sires with the existing native stock of 'running' horses which had been maintained at the royal studs since the reign of Henry VIII. The huge, international racing industry is based fair and square on the English Thoroughbred and follows the pattern established in Britain, although, of course, racing Thoroughbreds are now bred in every country in the world where the sport is carried on.

Up to the evolution of the Thoroughbred the greatest improving influence on the world's horse population was the Arabian, and after that the Barb and its probable derivative the Spanish horse, which we now tend to call Andalucian. However, once the Thoroughbred was established – and as a result of carefully documented selective breeding that happened in a remarkably short space of time – the Arab influence, although always powerful, went into gradual decline. Today, it is Thoroughbred blood which is regarded as the prime up-grading influence and an essential element in the production of competition horses.

Breeds, in the modern context, are a relatively recent innovation in equine history and there are very few stud books much more than a hundred years old. Indeed, just what constitutes a breed is not even a subject upon which there is universal agreement.

In the days before stud book registration a 'breed' would have constituted a group or groups of equines living in a particular region and which by reason of environment and the inevitable relationship between them displayed marked similarities in terms of conformation, coat-colour, height and general character.

Today, the title of 'breed' is given to a group of horses or ponies that have been selectively bred over a sufficient period to ensure the consistent production of stock sharing common and clearly defined characteristics. They must be the progeny of 'pure-bred' parents recorded in the stud book maintained by the breed society and, in turn, their progeny is entitled to be similarly registered. Technically, therefore, modern breeds date from Vol. 1 of their society's stud book, to which all registered animals must be traceable.

In fact, of course, breeds like the British native ponies, as much influenced by environment as human intervention, had been in the process of development long before anyone thought of putting them in a book.

Nonetheless, that definition now covers the British breeds, with the exception of the Irish Draught, which in England operates an up-grading register that will, in time, produce pure-bred, 'officially' registered stock. The other books are 'closed' stud books, which means that stock are only registered if both parents are in it.

This is not the situation in the countries of mainland Europe which, it has to be remembered have, during their history, suffered at first hand the effects of two world wars as well as numerous other earlier conflicts. In the course of those hostilities, or as a result of them, frontiers altered or disappeared, studs were broken up or changed hands, herds were dispersed and records lost. To some degree this is a reason for some European breed societies to operate an 'open' stud book system. This allows stock to be registered in the breed stud book so long as the parents are approved by the breed society and are themselves of pedigree stock: they do not have to be of the same breed. Many of the continental warm-bloods are a mix, although a controlled one, of a variety of bloods. Imported Thoroughbred and Arab are certainly there, whilst in some of the newer breeds there is a powerful Trakehner element, a breed established in what was East Prussia in the early eighteenth century. Often there is also evidence of both Cleveland and Hackney outcrosses.

The term warm-blood is of relatively recent origin and refers to the presence of Arab or more usually Thoroughbred blood. Both are termed as 'hot-bloods', whilst the heavy draught horses, descendants of Europe's primitive Forest or Diluvial horse, are known as 'cold-bloods'. In the past the term 'half-bred' was used to indicate a cross between a Thoroughbred and some other breed – pony, heavy horse or a horse of unknown pedigree. The progeny of a half-bred mare and a Thoroughbred horse would then be called 'three-quarter bred' and the progeny of a mare in that category crossed again to a Thoroughbred would be said to be 'seven-eighths bred'. These descriptions are still used in Britain, though the term warm-blood covers a horse carrying varying percentages of Thoroughbred blood.

'Part-bred' is another British word. It describes an animal that can claim a degree of relationship to an established breed, the percentage being laid down by the breed society concerned. Such animals are eligible for entry in a part-bred register; as examples there are part-bred Arabs, part-bred Welsh, Dartmoor and so on.

The 'open' stud book can also be regarded as a reflection of the pragmatism of continental breeding, which may be either state-controlled or state-supported, unlike the private enterprise system in Britain which depends on individuals breeding horses on a small scale without government encouragement. Countries like Germany, France, Holland and Denmark are concerned with the production of the purpose-bred horse, whether it is for dressage, showjumping or whatever. They mix bloods judiciously, adding a little of this or that to accentuate or maintain a particular feature. The Dutch Warm-blood is a case in point: it is to all intents an amalgam of the indigenous light draught horses, the Gelderland and Groningen, refined by the addition of Thoroughbred blood and then adjusted by the employment of related warm-blood stallions coming principally from France and Germany.

In some respects America is even more tolerant of out-crosses, and displays even less reverence for the sanctity of the British-pattern stud book. But we have to remember that in the space of less than two hundred years – a mere flicker of an eye-lid in an equine history which began millions of years before man assumed an upright stance – the American genius for adaptation has produced a whole variety of home-made breeds often possessed of unique characteristics, horses like the Tennessee Walker and the Missouri Fox-Trotter, for instance. Some of the American breeds, particularly the colour breeds, would not be accorded breed status in Britain because of the stock's lack of consistency in the essential characteristics. We should regard them as 'types' and do, indeed, consider the Palominos bred in Britain in that light.

Horse or pony 'types' are those that do not qualify as breeds because they lack fixed character. In Britain, hunters, hacks, polo ponies, cobs and even the British Riding Pony, which outside its country of origin would certainly be accorded breed status, are all classed as types. Nevertheless, they are far too important to be omitted altogether from this book, and they have therefore been grouped in a chapter of their own at the end.

This book makes its appearance as Britain enters fully into the European Economic Community, accepting all that implies in terms of the regulations which are common to all the member states. The essence of the Community is that it is a trading organisation and its regulations are designed to promote trade within and without the member states.

Those requirements are enormously complex and some have been vigorously opposed by Britain, in particular the removal of the minimum values legislation which protected horses and ponies from the cruelties involved in their being exported live for slaughter on the continent. That battle continues.

On the other hand, the harmonization of stud books, with the criteria for entry being laid down by the country of origin, has its advantages for British breeds, and so do the moves towards full documentation of all *equidae*, the word preferred by the EEC.

Many of the regulations offer increased opportunities for British breeders to promote the sale of stock throughout the market. That will be of obvious benefit to the breeds.

Whether the British breed societies are yet ready to provide the leadership and imagination that will be necessary to ensure success in Europe, and whether breeders are able to meet the challenges inherent in membership of the community still remains to be seen. What is certain is that they have the material to hand: they have now to recognise and exploit its potential within the wider concept of a very differently structured horse-world.

# 1

# *Nine Native Breeds –*
# *The Background*

The native or indigenous ponies of Britain and Ireland are just as frequently referred to as the Mountain and Moorland breeds. The title arises because the original habitat of the ponies was on those wild and sparsely populated areas stretching from Dartmoor and Exmoor in the south-west, up the western side of the country through the mountainous regions of Wales, and on northwards to the dales and fells along the Pennine chain. The rough land of Connemara, far to the west of Ireland, supported ponies, and in Scotland they were to be found on the Western Isles and Shetland as well as on the mainland. Yet another native breed came from that area of what is now Hampshire which is made up of wide stretches of moor and woodland and called the New Forest. Once the hunting ground of kings, it is still the largest parcel of unenclosed land in southern England.

Today, although there are no more truly feral stocks, ponies are still put out by their owners in all those areas, although all the nine surviving native breeds are also bred at studs throughout Britain as well as elsewhere in the world. Obviously, all these indigenous breeds have been refined, or perhaps 'modernized', by outcrossing and selective breeding, a process, indeed, which began before the Romans came to Britain.

There were once many more pony breeds native to the British Isles than the nine which are recognised today. There were the Lincolnshire Fen Ponies, unprepossessing maybe, but entirely suited to their wet and inhospitable environment; the enduring Cornish Goonhilly; the swift Irish Hobbys and Scottish Galloways, the latter the mounts of the Border raiders; and then the versatile Roadster from East Anglia who runs, or more correctly trots, like a golden thread through our equine history. These breeds became extinct either because they had no further practical use in a changing society, or they blended unobtrusively with other more fashionable blood and were absorbed, more often than not to the latter's great advantage. The Fen Pony, for instance, declined following the drainage of the Fens by Dutch engineers in the early seventeenth century and it had, indeed, suffered much degeneration long before that. The Galloway began to be absorbed into the Fell Pony in the eighteenth century soon after the disastrous Jacobite rising of '45 and had disappeared altogether in the following century.

Today, we are left with nine breeds: Exmoor, Dartmoor, New Forest, Welsh, Connemara, Dale, Fell, Highland and Shetland. They represent a unique group of equines and each retains a distinct character and appearance. Additionally, they inherit the hardiness, constitution and sagacity derived from their original environment, as well as an ability to survive and even thrive on the most sparse feed.

In 1912, when horsepower was still the essential element in the world economy, a government-appointed committee, formed to advise on what measures could be taken to improve the Mountain and Moorland breeds of ponies, had this to say ' . . . it is their emphatic and unanimous opinion that these ponies bred in the open are the natural reservoirs from which all our national breeds of light horses derive and reinvigorate many of their characteristics of temperament, courage and resource.'*

It does, indeed, appear that the British native ponies have very special qualities which are not found in other pony breeds and which reflect the natural vigour of their primitive ancestors – a vigour not nearly so evident in what may be termed the breeds 'invented' by man in his efforts to improve and adapt the natural elements to his own ends.

So what comprises the 'primitive' ancestry of this singular group of ponies? No one can provide a comprehensive answer to that, but we know enough about the evolution of the equine species, and about the changes in environment which have taken place during the sixty million years since the first horse ancestor emerged on the American continent, to perceive a pattern of development.

That first horse of the Dawn Period (Eocene) was called logically enough Eohippus, the Dawn Horse. Eohippus scarcely resembled the subsequent species we know as Equus, but it is possible to trace the latter's development from this animal of pre-history. Eohippus was a small, multi-toed animal, about the size of a dog or a fox, and probably had a striped or blotched coat so that it would blend into the forest background which was its habitat. By about a million years ago the single-foot species Equus had evolved in accordance with an environment which had changed during the Miocene period from being jungle swampland to treeless plains or steppe-lands supporting

Above: *A pair of sure-footed Dales Ponies, ideal mounts for riding over the wild Yorkshire uplands.*

Below: *The Exmoor breed thrives on the rough grasses of the moorland it has inhabited for thousands of years.*

a low growth of wiry grasses.

This species, *Equus Caballus*, spread via the existing land-bridges into South America and thence into Asia, Europe and Africa. The land-bridges were destroyed during the Ice Age, which extended from the Pleistocene period up to about 10,000 years ago. Then between 8-10,000 years ago the horse became extinct on the American continent in which it had evolved: at the same time the sloths and mastodons disappeared. How or why that happened is unknown to this day and we can only guess that it might have been due to some violent climatic change or to the incidence of some disease.

At that point there existed four closely related types of Equus: the horse, the ass, the zebra and the onager. The horse inhabited Europe and the nearer parts of Asia, the ass and zebra were to be found in the north and south of Africa respectively, whilst the onager belonged to the Middle East.

Environment is integral to the process of evolution and in Europe the temperate zones in which suitable feedstuff was readily available encouraged horses of greater size, the soil, rich in minerals and vitamins, contributing to their growth. Where there were conditions of high rainfall producing lush herbage a heavier, browsing type of animal evolved. Dry regions, in contrast, produced light-boned horses, not large but capable of swift movement. In mountainous regions where the rough ground supported no more than a sparse vegetation the animals were small and hardy and developed those

*Comparative body sizes of the horse and various ancestral forms.*

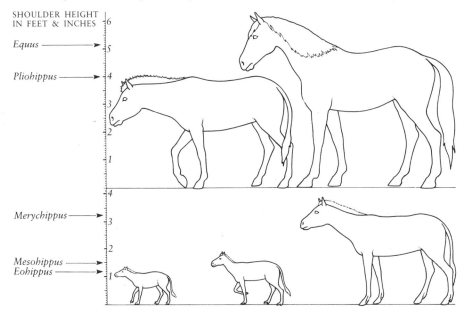

SHOULDER HEIGHT
IN FEET & INCHES

Equus

Pliohippus

Merychippus

Mesohippus
Eohippus

characteristics which enabled them to survive the harsh rigours of their habitat.

Out of these circumstances emerged three notable and well-defined horse types. These three 'founding fathers', which is what in essence they proved to be, were the Asiatic Wild Horse (*Equus Przewalskii Przewalskii Poliakov*), of Mongolia, which is now probably extinct in the wild but still exists in zoos throughout the world; the Plateau Horse with a habitat much further to the west, in eastern Europe and the Ukrainian steppes, which is called Tarpan (*Equus Przewalskii Gmelini Antonius*) and survives in a 'reconstituted' form in the famous Popielno herd in Poland; and the heavy, slow-moving *Przewalskii Silvaticus*, the Forest or Diluvial Horse, living in what were then the wet marshlands of northern Europe. It too is extinct in its original form.

A fourth horse type, the Tundra, inhabited that part of north-east Siberia where winter temperatures are below those at the North Pole. Scientific opinion is almost unanimous in holding that the Tundra had little or no influence on the evolution of the present-day domestic equine stock, although a connection to the Shetland pony is recognised.

In general terms it is not unreasonable to trace the ancestry of today's light horses from the Tarpan, which in slightly altered form becomes the Celtic or North Atlantic Pony, and the Asiatic Wild Horse stock via their subsequent derivatives; whilst the Forest Horse (possibly a derivative of the Asiatic Wild Horse) can be considered as the far-off ancestor of the heavy horse breeds.

Following that 'fundamentalist' view, the most favoured and publicised theory of evolution and also the most convenient, is that formulated by Professor Speed of Edinburgh and Professors Ebhardt and Skorkowski of Stuttgart and Cracow respectively, in the late nineteenth century, after their detailed analysis of bone structure and other characteristics. They concluded that immediately before domestication, which took place possibly 5-6000 years ago on the Eurasian steppes from whence derived a race of Indo-Europeans – later the Celtic people which came to occupy the western parts of Britain – there existed four equine types, two horse types and two pony.

> Pony Type 1, of north-west Europe, which is very similar to the modern Exmoor.
>
> Pony Type 2, a bigger specimen living in northern Eurasia. After the Asiatic Wild Horse the Highland pony is the modern equivalent.
>
> Horse Type 3, taller, up to 14.3 h.h. long and narrow. Habitat

Central Asia. Modern equivalent the desert Akhal-Teke of Turkmenistan.

Horse Type 4, smaller but very refined, living in western Asia, the prototype Arabian exemplified by the Caspian Pony.

The division between horse and pony is usually arbitrarily defined today by height – under 15 h.h. is a pony and over that height a horse. However, that assumption is incorrect: it is really all to do with proportion, which is why an Arab, for instance, is a horse, even though it stands no more than 14.2 h.h.

The founding fathers and these subsequent sub-types had evolved long before the British Isles had separated from the European continent. Furthermore no one type could have remained inviolate – cross-breeding has to have been inevitable. It is, therefore, not unreasonable to assume that after the Ice Age which created the British Isles as a separate entity, divided by the Channel and the North Sea from mainland Europe and from Ireland by another expanse of water, the equine population consisted of Pony Type 1 and $1 \times 4$, introducing the Plateau element, and heavier specimens from Type 2 or $1 \times 2$.

The last land-bridge, from the Scilly Isles, broke down around 15,000 BC in the Old Stone Age, and no new additions to the British equine population could be made for some 14,000 years. Not until the Bronze Age, somewhere around 1000 BC, were men able to make ships big enough and strong enough to transport horses and cattle. From that point there is evidence of horses being brought to Britain from Scandinavia. Almost certainly, the Shetland came from those parts, its diminutive stature being fixed by the relative isolation of the Shetland Isles, which prohibited any out-cross, as well as by the environment. Dales, Fells and Highlands would all have benefited from stock brought in by marauders from Scandinavia at this time and later in history, but it is not until the Roman occupation that we have significant out-crosses of Oriental blood when the Phoenicians brought in eastern horses on their western trading routes.

The Romans certainly brought in Friesian horses which had an undoubted influence on the Dales and Fell Ponies. The most interesting of their military settlements from a horse viewpoint is that at Trimontium, now known as Newstead, near Melrose in Roxburghshire. The site, big enough to accommodate a Legion, was first occupied during Agricola's Caledonian expedition in AD 73. There may have been as many as 1000 horses of all types housed here and Professor J. Cossar Ewart, the foremost of the modern British hippologists, showed, following an examination of the site and the remains found on it, the existence of six principal types of pony as well as a number of intermediate cross-breds. One type resembling a Tarpan he termed Celtic; another was a Shetland; there were two types similar to the modern Exmoor, one with Arab characteristics and the other rather heavier and more inclined towards a Forest (Diluvial) conformation. There were also horses of about 14 h.h., indistinguishable from modern Arabians of desert breeding, and lastly some bigger horses with very heavy, coarse heads which could have been of German origin. Otherwise, the Celtic type predominated.

This then was the melting pot from which, in time, emerged the British Mountain and Moorland population, each breed developing, and sometimes degenerating, in accordance with environmental pressures and those exerted by the needs of man.

The native breeds were employed in all sorts of capacities right up to the end of the nineteenth century and beyond. They supported the Industrial Revolution as pit ponies; they worked for small traders and on milk rounds and in delivery vans in the towns and cities, and they provided the Army with the sinews of war. Shetlands worked on crofts, Dales and Fells as pack ponies, and even more natives, particularly the Welsh, were employed on farms as maids-of-all-work. They provided a base for crossing, producing, for instance, the unique Riding Pony, whilst many good jumpers and hunters also had

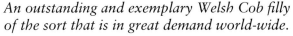

*An outstanding and exemplary Welsh Cob filly*
*of the sort that is in great demand world-wide.*

the background of native blood.

Since then, as refinements were made, often because of the introduction of Arab blood, they were exported extensively. Only the Shetland has really remained pure, for it does not cross easily even though there is an American Shetland, the result of a large infusion of Hackney blood.

The watershed in the development of the modern Mountain and Moorlands dates from the establishment of the breed societies and the opening of stud books. The principal dates are these:

1890   Formation of Shetland Pony Stud Book Society.

1898   Formation of committees organised by the Polo and Riding Pony Society (later the National Pony Society) to study native breeds.

1899   Native sections opened in the Stud Book of the above society.

1901   Formation of the Welsh Pony and Cob Society (Stud Book Vol. 1 published 1902).

1910   First Stud Book of the Burley and District New Forest Pony and Cattle Society.

1916   Dales Pony recognised as being distinct from Fell and breed society formed.

1920   Fell Pony Society formed.

1921   Exmoor Pony Society formed.

1923   Highland Pony Society formed.

1923   Connemara Pony Breeders' Society (Ireland) formed.

1924   Dartmoor Pony Society formed following demise of an earlier association.

1947   English Connemara Pony Society formed.

Today's ponies are used extensively for riding and driving and as a foundation for crossing. They remain the 'natural reservoirs' reinvigorating the 'characteristics of temperament, courage and resource' and they are unmatched in every respect by any ponies bred elsewhere in the world.

* Report of the Board of Agriculture and Fisheries Committee appointed in 1912 to advise upon methods of improvement relative to the Mountain and Moorland breeds.

# 2

# *The Exmoor*

The Exmoor is the oldest breed of British native pony and its origins are probably as ancient as any of today's equine races. It takes its name from its natural habitat in the western part of Somerset, the high, bleak, windswept plateau of Exmoor, the smallest of the National Parks. Here the rainfall is high and the area, intersected with swift-running rivers, abounds in the steep valleys known in the West Country as combes. Vegetation on the higher land consists almost entirely of rough grasses, heather and bracken. The latter is poisonous to cattle and sheep, but the ponies and the wild deer eat the shoots with no ill effect and in the winter paw up the bracken and cotton grass to feed on the starch-filled tubers.

Not all the ponies to be seen on the Moor are pure-bred: there are mixed herds on the Withypool, Molland and Brendon Commons, for instance, and numbers of scrub stock elsewhere, that is, degenerate stock of mixed, promiscuous breeding. The pure-bred Exmoors are pretty well confined to the areas encompassing Ashway Side, Winsford Hill, Codsend Moor and Cheriton Ridge. There are three principal herds on Exmoor itself and the ponies are also bred in a small way at studs elsewhere in the country. Ponies bred away from the Moor, however, tend to lose type, and breeders find it necessary to return to the original Exmoor stock to maintain the essential character.

The principal ancestor of the Exmoor is that primitive Pony Type 1 discussed in the previous chapter, which had evolved thousands of years before the British Isles were separated from the European mainland. Remains of this early equine, discovered in Alaska and dated as belonging to the Pleistocene age two million years ago, match the bone structure and, in particular, the unique jaw formation of the modern Exmoor, which shows the beginnings of a seventh molar tooth not found in any other equine. The record of their movement following the thaw of the Alaskan glaciers is revealed in prehistoric rock paintings in the Ural mountains and a trail of fossilised and sub-fossilised remains which lead to the south-west of England – then connected to mainland Europe by dry land – via Romania, Austria, Germany and France.

There is a wealth of archaeological evidence showing that Exmoor ponies were employed in chariots during the Bronze Age, and this period in the history of the breed produced a peculiar conformational feature which persisted into modern times. Early chariot harness was based on adaptations of the yoke principle which had been developed for oxen long before the equine was used in draught. The lightweight chariot was pulled from a broad strap encircling the front part of the pony's neck. Since a pair of ponies or more could be harnessed to a single chariot the tractive arrangement worked well enough, but in consequence the ponies developed a pronounced muscular bulge on the under-side of the neck. In time this development was eradicated, but it is remarkable that it should appear in stock separated from the original cause of the deformity by so long a period of time.

In Roman Britain the Exmoor became a saddle horse. There is a Romano-British carved slab of about the second century at the Dorchester Museum which shows clearly a Thracian rider-god on what is unmistakably an Exmoor pony, 'toad' eyes and all. The Exmoor is depicted again on the Bayeux Tapestry recording the arrival of William the Conqueror in Britain in 1066. The Domesday Book of AD 1085 refers to the presence of 104 brood mares in the manor of Brendon and 72 at Lynton.

From Norman times up to the early part of the nineteenth century Exmoor was a Royal Forest with local people holding grazing rights. Exmoor was disafforested and partly enclosed in 1818, a date that became a landmark in the breed's development. At that point two famous herds came into being, those of Sir Thomas Acland and Mr John Knight, a Worcestershire industrialist who by 1820 owned some 15,000 acres around Simonsbath. The latter pursued a policy of improving or breeding up his Exmoor stock, using, not entirely satisfactorily, a Dongola horse of Barb origin which stood around 16 h.h. Mr Knight (later Sir John) died in 1850 and a decade later his son Frederick, who followed his father's breeding policy, had established with the help of Welsh Cob crosses what people talked about as the Exmoor Cob, a type reminiscent of the pack ponies which were much used in the area, though much improved.

The Knights' 'improved' stock had no lasting effect upon the pure Exmoor and passed into oblivion in a relatively short time. It was the Acland ponies, known as the Anchor herd because of the distinctive brand mark, which preserved the essential characteristics of the old

*The wild, high plateau of Exmoor in south-west Britain
is the natural home for the pony herds.*

native breed, and the Anchor herd is still the principal influence in the Exmoor today.

Sir Thomas Acland, writing in 1886, stated that in 1815, just before the disafforestation, his father had about five hundred ponies running wild on the Moor and he mentions that a famous stallion, Katerfelto, was supposed to have been responsible for introducing either Arab or Spanish blood into the herds. Katerfelto, the title of one of Whyte Melville's novels, was described by G.S. Lowe in his book *The Horses of the British Empire* (1907) as 'a sort of spectre horse constantly seen on the moors, but no one knew where he came from'. He was eventually captured and was described as being a dun horse of about 14 h.h. with a black list (stripe) down his back. There are other versions of the Katerfelto legend but the truth of it is unlikely ever to be known. However, if the description is correct the dun colouring points to a Spanish horse, since it is not found in the Arab.

The Aclands kept a private stud book but unfortunately it was lost in a fire during the Second World War. It was re-opened in 1952, but it was not until ten years later that the Exmoor Pony Society published its own Stud Book. Up to that time all entries were made through the National Pony Society.

To be eligible for registration in the Stud Book, an Exmoor pony, as well as being the progeny of registered parents, must be inspected by the Society's officials. Their examination is based upon type, conformation, soundness and accepted colour, and any suspicion of white in the coat or the hooves is a sufficient reason for rejection since it is regarded as evidence of alien blood. Colts are examined again at two years old to decide whether they are suitable for use as stallions. All ponies accepted for registration are branded with the Society's star above the herd number.

The Exmoor breed, as might be expected of one of such ancient origin, is distinctive in appearance, although there is a division in type between the Acland (Anchor) and the ponies of the Withypool pure-bred herd, the latter being a little bigger and with a noticeably straighter profile.

The Exmoor colours are bay, brown or dun with a characteristic 'mealy' colouring round the eyes, the muzzle and on the inner flanks. Dun, in the Exmoor context, is not the expected fawn-yellow but a slate-coloured grey not dissimilar to the primitive Tarpan in colouring. In summer, buff-coloured markings appear in the coat but white hairs are not permissible. The official standard of the Exmoor Pony Society stipulates a height not exceeding 12.3 h.h. for stallions and geldings and not exceeding 12.2 h.h. for mares.

Unique features of the Exmoor are the hooded 'toad' eye; the 'ice' tail, with an additional thick and fan-like growth at the top, and the double-textured coat. In winter the latter is thick, harsh and springy, providing an entirely weatherproof covering. In summer the texture becomes close and hard, assuming a particular metallic sheen. The Exmoor head is somewhat larger in its proportion than that of other breeds, supposedly because the nasal passages, rather like those of the Shetland, are longer so that cold air has a chance to be warmed before reaching the lungs. These 'primitive' characteristics are the result of environmental pressures exerted since prehistoric times and which have been retained because of the isolation and severity of the moorland habitat.

The Exmoor is a strong, robust, well-balanced pony and capable of carrying weight out of proportion to its size. As a hunting pony the Exmoor was, and still is, capable of carrying a full-grown man. William Youatt, the nineteenth-century authority and author of *The Different Breeds of English Horses* (c.1820), writes about 'a well-known sportsman' who rode an Exmoor and 'never felt such power and action in so small a compass'. That pony cleared a gate eight inches higher than himself and was said to have carried his 14-stone (196lb) owner the 86 miles from Bristol to South Molton in less time than the fast stage-coach of the day. As a hunter for a keen child or a light adult the Exmoor today, if properly schooled, would be hard to beat and, like the breed's Bronze Age ancestors, it is still a formidable performer in harness.

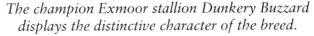

*The champion Exmoor stallion Dunkery Buzzard displays the distinctive character of the breed.*

*Swift-running rivers, intersecting the moorland*

*...old no terrors for the Exmoor ponies.*

As foundation stock for breeding bigger horses it is not perhaps sufficiently appreciated. The legendary hunting parson, the Reverende John Russell, (immortalised by the Jack Russell terriers which he bred and which are named after him) used to say that no hunter was any good without having a percentage of Exmoor blood. He held that the best hunter – in the modern context we could use the term 'competition' horse – was bred by a Thoroughbred sire out of a Thoroughbred/Exmoor cross dam. G.S. Lowe commented: 'Such a bred one would stay for ever, be as intelligent as a dog, the pony strain would ensure that, and he would last as well – Parson Jack Russell would have said twenty years at two days hunting a week.' He was probably right: The Colonel, winner of the Grand National in 1869 and 1870, was sired by a part-bred Exmoor, and New Oswestry, sire of the 1883 winner Zoedone, also had Exmoor blood.

In a sense, today's sadly depleted Exmoor herds remain as nearly wild as it is possible to be in the late twentieth century. They are 'gathered' in October and driven to their owners' farms to be inspected and for selected foals intended for sale to be separated. The 'gathering' lasts about a fortnight after which the herds return to the moor, and in general this is the only contact they have with humans. For this reason the ponies are naturally nervous of encounters with people or, indeed, dogs, and they are the only British breed which has ever been observed to react to the primitive 'wolf alert'. On the approach of a large dog, or even a group of riders, the herds have been seen to take up a defensive position prompted, it must be presumed, by some atavistic memory. The ponies form a tight circle with the foals in the centre. The adults face inwards presenting a wall of hind feet at the ready to repulse any attack. The whole formation then revolves slowly on its axis while the herd stallion faces the danger from outside the circle, which protects his rear. He is then ready to attack with striking fore-feet or to savage an assailant with his teeth.

After the autumn inspections it has been customary for surplus colt foals, that is those not considered suitable to be retained for breeding, to be sold either to private owners or at that traditional venue provided by Bampton Fair. In times when the Exmoor was numerous the sale yards were full of young, unhandled ponies driven to the Fair in herds. Just after the Second World War as many as three hundred foals were sold at Bampton each year – over half of the estimated Exmoor pony population today!

The sale of the foals was a necessity for the farmers who ran herds on the Exmoor 'allotments', since the supply of fodder would support no more than a limited number. Whether the practice acted to the benefit of the breed is less certain, for it contributed to the Exmoor's reputation for being wild, difficult and unsuitable for children. Of course, the frightened foals, that had never been haltered, were hardly an attractive proposition as potential mounts for children and, indeed, those that were later broken were often roughly handled.

The Exmoor never was a child's first pony, it is far too quick and highly-couraged for that, and it is also of an independent disposition. However, if that is taken into account and a sympathetic trainer bears in mind the pony's natural wariness of humans and their ways, the Exmoor can be a brilliant performer for an older child.

Today, there is much concern about the future of the Exmoor, and numbers have reached so dangerously low a level that the Rare Breeds Survival Trust has categorised the breed as being in danger of extinction (i.e. Category 1, 'critical'). It is thought possibly that no more than five hundred survive worldwide. One factor, unappreciated perhaps by those who seek to ban field sports, is that the ponies and the red deer are to a great degree inter-dependent because they live on the same foodstuffs. Deer hunting is traditional to the Moor and acts as a cull on excessive numbers. When during the wars it was not carried out the red deer became nearly extinct as a result of indiscriminate shooting. If hunting was banned, the farmers would be inclined to eliminate the deer as pests causing damage to their crops. If the deer went and their natural habitat became enclosed and thus denied to the ponies, the future of the latter would in the view of many practical conservationists be put at great risk.

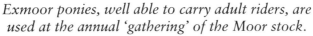

*Exmoor ponies, well able to carry adult riders, are
used at the annual 'gathering' of the Moor stock.*

Above: *'Gathering' the ponies for inspection by the Society officials takes place annually in October.*

Left: *Only ponies like those of Exmoor can withstand the hardships of winter on the moorland.*

Right: *An Exmoor in his weatherproof winter coat is well able to withstand the harshest weather.*

# 3

# *The Dartmoor*

Because access to its wild environment was difficult, the Exmoor pony remained relatively untainted by 'improving' zealotry and alien blood. It might be thought that the neighbouring Dartmoor herds would be just as immune from outside influence and perhaps even more so, in view of their location further to the south of Exmoor's wild and windy plateau. A closer examination of the map, however, reveals why this was not the case.

The raiding Danes sailed up the Tamar and other rivers of the south-west coast in the ninth century and brought with them the stallions they rode. Both Exeter and Plymouth, the two major towns of the south-west, were of ancient foundation, Exeter being established by the Romans, whilst Plymouth was certainly of major importance in the Middle Ages. The direct route between the two lay across the rough moorland, and afforded ample opportunity for the infusion of all sorts of outside blood into the Dartmoor herds. There was no comparable route across Exmoor and no port there with links to the Continent.

The first mention of the Dartmoor stock appears in 1012 in the will of a Saxon bishop, Aefwold of Crediton, when a group was bequeathed to religious houses in the area. Oriental blood was probably introduced in the reign of Henry I (1100-1135) and more Eastern blood may have come in with the returning Crusaders in the same century. Henry had received a gift of two Eastern horses from Europe and stood a stallion at the royal manor of Gillingham to serve his own mares. It seems possible that one of these gift horses was used. Up to the end of the nineteenth century outside blood was introduced in great variety: cobs, from Wales and elsewhere; Hackney, of the Roadster sort; Arab or Barb; small Thoroughbred and other native ponies, including, naturally, some Exmoor, whilst in the background was the old and now long-forgotten Devon Pack

Horse, itself drawing from both Exmoor and Dartmoor blood, and, of course, the extinct Goonhilly Pony of Cornwall.

To what extent the outside crosses made in the earlier part of the nineteenth century influenced the breed's development is questionable since the best of the resultant progeny, those of Thoroughbred or Arab parentage, were probably sold 'up-country' and would have had no subsequent effect.

William Youatt, never one to flatter, wrote in 1820: 'There is on Dartmoor a race of ponies much in request in that vicinity, being sure-footed and hardy and admirably calculated to scramble over the rough roads and dreary wilds of that mountainous district. The Dartmoor is larger than the Exmoor and, if possible, uglier. He exists there almost in a state of nature.' Fifty-odd years later *The Field*, discussing crosses made from moor stock, commented on their speed, activity, staying power and inherent soundness, remarking that 'they can jump as well as the moor sheep and much after the same fashion, for no hedge or fence can stop either one or the other' – which, it may be noted, implies the possession of good riding shoulders and much strength in the back and loins.

For all that, the tough Dartmoor pony of good riding type had almost disappeared during the peak years of the Industrial Revolution when Shetland stallions were turned on the moor with the object of producing pit ponies. It was a disastrous experiment from which the breed was saved largely by the intervention of the Polo and Riding Pony Society, founded in 1893 and soon to take on its modern title of National Pony Society. The Society opened a Dartmoor section in the Stud Book and encouraged the use of quality pony stallions to upgrade the moor stock. It has always been held, and it is recorded by authorities like Sir Walter Gilbey and Lord Arthur Cecil, that Welsh Mountain ponies were in the van of this drive to exert an improving influence, and Welsh breeders in general support the assertion. But in Dartmoor records, those within the section maintained in the NPS Stud Book from 1899 to 1914, it appears that only one pony is credited with Welsh ancestry. However, the documentation of the Dartmoor breed, as well as others, at that period was incomplete and it could be that some Welsh stock was being introduced by the 'moormen'. Whatever the truth of it there is still a suggestion, if no more, of Welsh ancestry in the appearance of the Dartmoor. Apart from the Fell, Mikado, the greatest influences in the early part of this century were the polo pony stallions Lord Polo, a son of Sir Humphrey de Trafford's Rosewater, a Thoroughbred and the foundation sire of the British polo pony, and Punchinello, who was by an Arab but could have had Welsh antecedents on the dam's side.

Above: *The long, low action of the Dartmoor is a notable feature among the pony breeds. Left: This Dartmoor mare and foal belong to one of the few pure-* bred herds still running on the moor.
Below: *An evocative snow-scene, featuring hardy Dartmoor ponies, that has a Christmas card quality.*

A century or so ago there were three distinct herds on the moor. The herd in the south-west was dark brown with light mealy muzzles; that near South Zeal was bay, sometimes described as rose bay, and the third, all greys, belonged by long tradition to Sourton Common. Today's Dartmoors are for the most part produced on private studs throughout Britain and grey would now be a most unusual colour, bay and brown being predominant.

Without any doubt the two greatest factors in the development of the modern Dartmoor were the stallion called The Leat and his remarkable owner Miss Sylvia Calmady-Hamlyn who was Honorary Secretary of the Dartmoor Pony Society for 32 years and re-formed the Society with her friend Miss Dawson in 1923-24 a short time after she turned from breeding polo ponies to pure Dartmoors.

The Leat was not pure-bred. His sire was Dwarka, a desert-bred Arab who had raced successfully in India, and his dam was the black 13 h.h. mare Blackdown by Confident George out of a Dartmoor mare. The Leat was bred in 1918 by the Prince of Wales at Tor Royal, whilst Blackdown was bred by Mrs Crocker of the *Plume of Feathers*, Princetown.

The Leat was described as 'a magnificent pony' with a beautiful head, excellent shoulders and exemplary hindlegs. He was 12.2 h.h. and though he was at stud for only three years his descendants are still the most predominant in Dartmoor breeding. He founded two principal lines, the first from Judy V and the second from Scintilla.

Judy V was the dam of Juliet IV (by The Leat) and she when put to the Welsh Mountain Pony Dinarth Spark was the dam of the most famous Dartmoor stallion of them all, Jude.

Scintilla's exceptional daughters by The Leat were Sparklet II and Water Wagtail. Sparklet's son, the champion Boxer, by The Leat, sired Queenie XXIII, the dam of a number of well-known Dartmoors. This line avoids entirely the influence of Dinarth Spark. Wagtail was the dam of the famous Peewit III, by Spark and she produced the stallion Pipit when put to Jude.

By the end of the Second World War, when the moor was used as an army training area, the Dartmoor was once more close to extinction, and in 1941-43 only two males and twelve females were offered for registration. Miraculously the breed was saved again by the efforts of a few dedicated breeders.

There are a few herds of pure-bred Dartmoors still on the moor owned by breeders like the Coakers, whose Sherberton prefix is one of the oldest in the Dartmoor annals. Many of the ponies to be seen, however, are no more than scrub stock of mixed breeding with little to do with the pure Dartmoor strains and with no connection to the Dartmoor Pony Society. Their neglect in recent years has been little short of a national scandal, the often emaciated ponies suffering great hardship and even death in the rigours of the winter weather.

After so checkered a history and so disparate an amalgam of contributing bloods, it is remarkable that the end-product should be one of the most elegant riding ponies in the world, fixed in type and with all the essential pony characteristics: constitutional hardiness, good temperament, inherent soundness, little prick ears and all – the latter being a feature of the real 'pony', the opposite betraying the presence of an unwanted outside agency.

With the Welsh, the Dartmoor has dominated the riding pony classes and has contributed very significantly to that near perfectly proportioned equine, the British Riding Pony. It is very popular on the Continent, even being raced in Belgium, and it jumps as well as its forebears, but now with more scope. It is a wonderful cross with the Thoroughbred and the Arab, the second cross with the former being calculated to produce a top cross-country horse or hunter, and it has a most equable temperament, a vital factor in pony breeding.

The height of the modern Dartmoor is limited to 12.2 h.h. No colours are barred, other than skewbald or piebald, but bay, black and brown are preferred by exhibitors. The action, on account of those good shoulders, is notable amongst the pony breeds. It is low and long and economical – 'typical hack or riding action' as the breed standard states.

*Mrs. Jones and Miss Roberts' Champion Dartmoor White Willows Darwin, National Pony Show 1982.*

*The Dartmoor Horton Nimbus. Dartmoors are among the world's most elegant riding ponies*

*A study of a Dartmoor head that is revealing of the breed's character and intelligence.*

# 4

# *The New Forest Pony*

The original habitats of the majority of the British Mountain and Moorland breeds were in the country's less accessible areas. In consequence, outside influences, other than those deliberately introduced, were limited.

This was not the case with the New Forest Pony, colloquially termed the Forester. The original habitat of the breed before the Norman Conquest would have extended right across Southern England from east of Southampton up to Dartmoor and even to the fringes of Exmoor. It is not therefore unreasonable to assume that the breeds of Southern England sprang from a common root.

In time cultivations separated the three areas. Dartmoor and Exmoor were more or less isolated, but the tract of land in south-west Hampshire which is the New Forest, although huge in extent, was far more accessible because of its position on the routes leading to Winchester, then England's capital city, and the west. As a result there were limitless opportunities for the Forest ponies to be crossed with domestic stock of all kinds, whether resident about the area or passing through the Forest. As the Forest became increasingly traversed by tracks and roadways, access became even easier and the ability to introduce outside blood to the herds increased accordingly.

We know from the Forest Law of King Canute, proclaimed at Winchester in 1016, that ponies as well as cattle and pigs lived in the Forest at that time and it must be presumed that by then they were well-established.

Following the Norman Conquest, William Rufus made the Forest a royal hunting ground in which the deer were protected by severe and strictly enforced laws, but from earliest times the Right of Common Pasture was extended to those occupying Forest land. It still holds good today when the present-day Commoners continue to exercise their right to graze stock in the Forest.

The Commoners are represented by the Court of Verderers (fifty per cent of whose members are elected by the Commoners), and this body is responsible for the welfare and improvement of the Forest stock, control and inspection of stallions and also for the overall administration of the Forest. To carry out the practical day-to-day management the Verderers appoint three full-time agisters, whose duties include tail-marking the ponies to identify the districts in which they are turned out.

The earliest record of an attempt to upgrade the Forest stock dates back as far as 1208 when eighteen Welsh mares were introduced, and, in common with nearly all the British native breeds, the Forest ponies are supposed to have benefited from those ubiquitous equine survivors of the wrecked Spanish Armada in the sixteenth century. There is no more evidence to substantiate this last tale so far as the New Forest Pony is concerned than there is for any other native strain and it can be discounted.

What is certain is that in 1765, following the dispersal of the Duke of Cumberland's studs, the Thoroughbred Marske was acquired by a Dorset farmer and used on the Forest ponies. At a time when the average height for Thoroughbreds was around 14 h.h., Marske, a horse who ran with no success on the turf, stood at certainly no more than 14.2 h.h. He was at stud in the Forest area until his son, Eclipse, probably the greatest racehorse of all time, began his remarkable career, establishing an awesome reputation in the course of his first racing season in 1769. Marske was promptly rescued from obscurity and moved to Yorkshire where he continued his stud career in a manner more befitting the sire of such a prodigy.

Sir Walter Gilbey in his book *Thoroughbred and Other Ponies* (1900) wrote that between 1765-69, 'The New Forest breed of ponies was being improved by the very best Thoroughbred blood, the effects of which continued to be apparent for many years after Marske had left the district.' Marske, however, served only selected mares and the long-term effect of his particular contribution to the Forest stock is possibly more debatable.

Some form of selective breeding may have been practised by the Commoners in the following years but it was not until the nineteenth century that further positive action was taken to improve the Foresters. In 1852 Queen Victoria lent the Verderers the Arab stallion Zorah, but in four years he covered no more than 112 selected mares and his influence was, therefore, no more than minimal. By 1885 concern was being expressed about the deterioration of the stock, largely because of continual in-breeding within the herds. To correct the situation the Verderers hired four 'well-bred' stallions, but funds ran out and after two years the stallions had to go. The

Above: *A typical Forest mare with a young foal born within the natural environment of the New Forest.*

Right: *The modern New Forest Pony has the size, scope and ability to excel in competitive events.*

*Docility, common-sense and intelligence are hallmarks of the New Forest breed, however young.*

implementation of a stallion premium scheme in 1889, by which premium winners were required to be run in the forest from the show date in April up to August helped matters considerably and in the same year, the Queen again lent two stallions, the Arab Abeyan, and the Barb Yirrassan. They stood for two and three seasons respectively, the former exerting a considerable influence through a son out of a Welsh mare, a stallion that was, says Sir Walter Gilbey, 'in eager demand among the Commoners'.

The salvation of the Forester and without any doubt the greatest factor in the development of the modern pony was the beneficial intervention of Lord Arthur Cecil and later of Lord Lucas, both of whom were landowners in and about the Forest. Cecil and Lucas were instrumental in the formation in 1891 of the Association for the Improvement of the Breed of New Forest Ponies and then, in 1906, of the Burley and District New Forest Pony and Cattle Society, the body which published the first stud book in 1910, and of which Lucas was the first chairman.

Cecil was one of the most respected authorities of the day and his reputation, like that of his contemporary Sir Walter Gilbey, remains undiminished by the passage of time. He determined upon a seemingly radical solution designed to correct the Forest pony's deficiencies in respect of bone, substance and hardiness. He introduced a veritable *pot-pourri* of kindred native bloods and in massive proportions. There were the Rhum ponies (the Highland strain known as Black Galloways), Fells, Dales, Dartmoors, Exmoors, Welsh, of course, and still more Highlands. Lucas was responsible for the introduction of the famous Welsh Starlight blood, running out Picket Daylight (by Dyoll Starlight) and Picket Grayling (by Starlight's son Greylight) and a whole lot more Picket ponies carrying not only Welsh, but Fell, Dartmoor and Exmoor blood.

Lord Lucas died in 1916 on active service, three years after the death of his friend Cecil, having previously gone to the Boer War with the New Forest Scouts, all of them mounted on New Forest ponies. After losing a leg in South Africa he had brought back with him a Basuto stallion, admiring the versatility and inbred toughness of the breed. Lucas, a great if sometimes unconventional improver, certainly used the Basuto on Forest mares, though little if anything is known about the progeny.

The Basuto apart, the introduction of native blood in such variety and quantity might be thought to preclude the establishment of a discernible fixed type, and indeed, it is still possible to detect elements of other native breeds in the Foresters. But such is the influence of the environment, that 'mysterious power of nature to grind down and assimilate all these types to the one most suited to the land', as Lord

Arthur Cecil observed, that a distinctive type did emerge in the end, a process accelerated by the Society's ban on further infusions of outside blood made in the 1930s.

After the Second World War a group of Forest-bred stallions emerged as a major influence and they are recognised as the foundation sires of the modern breed. In the background, however, is the very important Field Marshal, a polo pony stallion out of a Welsh mare, who stood in the Forest in 1918-19. He was in the lines of many of the famous Brookside ponies.

The foundation stallions, which will be found in the pedigrees of the great majority of the best Foresters, were Denny Danny, with a direct line to Starlight blood and very Welsh in appearance; Goodenough, whose sire was unknown, but was from a Welsh-type dam reputed to be by Field Marshal; Brooming Slipon, a red chestnut by Telegraph Rocketer out of the mare Judy XV; Brookside David, a big, wall-eyed pony by Brookside Firelight who was descended from Field Marshal, and Knightwood Spitfire, the last of the foundation group, by Brookside Spitfire out of Weirs Topsy, a mare by the black Highland, Clansman, from whom all dun Foresters are said to descend.

Whether a *distinctive* type can be regarded as *fixed* is problematical, for of all the native breeds the Forester is the one more subject to variation than any other, particularly, of course, in regard to height. Some of the Forest-bred ponies may be as small as 12 or 12.2 h.h. whilst the stud-bred Foresters, certainly one of the most commercially viable of the British ponies, will reach the maximum permitted height of 14.2 h.h. Any colours, other than piebald, skewbald and blue-eyed cream, are acceptable in the breed.

What is without doubt distinctive is the special character of New Forest ponies and their way of moving, both of which they inherit very largely from their environment. Like all the native breeds they are naturally sure-footed, but they have a length of stride which is not so usually found in other pony breeds. Without much doubt, however, the canter is the Forester's best pace and the least tiring one to cross the open moorland with its thick cover of strong-growing heather. The trot is much less frequently employed, the ponies often moving directly into canter from the walk.

Sometimes the heads of the Foresters may be rather large, even horsy, and the Forest-bred stock may droop in the quarters. But these faults are offset by the almost universal well-sloped riding shoulder and a quite remarkable ability to perform in every sort of discipline at an above average level.

Temperamentally, the Forester is an ideal mount for both adults and children. Less sharp, or cunning, than some other native breeds, one or two of which have their 'wild' strains, the Forest pony is docile, highly intelligent and possessed of a lot of common sense. The temperament, whether the ponies are run in the Forest or are bred in more controlled stud conditions, derives from generations of ponies who lived naturally in close and regular contact with humans. They are as a result more easily handled than breeds whose early lives are spent on the hills and who have had little opportunity to become accustomed to man and his ways. In addition, since the Forest ponies are accustomed to traffic passing through and across the Forest, it is very rare to find a New Forest pony which takes the slightest notice of even the largest vehicles.

The Forester on all these counts, and in particular because of its outstanding versatility, is in great demand as a riding pony of size and substance. It excels in harness, long-distance riding, jumping and polo, and it is also raced enthusiastically over fences on its native heath.

Feed in the Forest is sufficient without being abundant. It comprises purple moor grass, which grows around the numerous bogs which are a feature of the terrain; other coarse grasses; water sweet grass, sedge, rushes; bramble leaves and tree shoots and gorse, which is a particular favourite. Gorse tips are highly nutritious and the ponies have developed special skills to deal with this prickly food. In some areas of the Forest where gorse is plentiful ponies have adapted to the situation by growing a wiry moustache on the upper lip and sometimes the suggestion of a beard on the lower jaw.

The breed society is the New Forest Pony Breeding and Cattle Society which was formed in 1938 as a result of the amalgamation of the Association for the Improvement of the Breed of New Forest Ponies (founded 1891) and the Burley and District New Forest Pony and Cattle Society (1906). This last Society produced stud books in 1910 and 1912 but thereafter registrations were included in the stud books of the National Pony Society. The New Forest Pony Breeding and Cattle Society produced its own stud book in 1960.

Sales of New Forest ponies are held at Beaulieu Road, the first one, from which foals are expressly excluded, taking place in April. Ponies living on the Forest are sold at the August sale and this is followed by two sales in September, two in October and one in November. The bulk of the foals are sold at the last five sales.

Beaulieu Road, successor to the sales held at Martinstown Fair, Dorset, and at Ringwood, Lyndhurst and Brockenhurst, was first used in 1941 and has now become part of the Forest's way of life. It is in every sense a country affair attracting crowds of buyers and onlookers, of course, but providing one of the year's highlights for the Commoners and their families, who follow the sale of their own

Above: *The autumn 'pony drifts', when stock are branded and tail-marked, are a feature of Forest life.*

Below: *During the 'drift' ponies are driven by mounted men into strategically placed pounds.*

and their neighbours' animals with keen attention and appropriate comment.

Nonetheless, the sales have also attracted adverse criticism on account of the conditions and the rough handling the ponies sometimes receive, even to the extent of questions being asked in the House of Commons. A percentage of the complaints come from the soft-hearted but largely unknowledgeable spectators holidaying in the area and can be discounted to a degree. Some, however, are justified and in recent years the Commoners have also, on more than one occasion, been accused of neglecting the Forest stock, provoking strong criticism in the press and causing concern to the animal welfare agencies.

As recently as 1991 the British Horse Society stated that it was 'horrified' at the 'deplorable standards of pony management in the New Forest'. It claimed that the ponies' plight weakened the British campaign to improve equine welfare standards in Europe and in a subsequent statement said:

> The ponies, whilst living in a semi-wild state, are not truly wild. They have owners who are failing in their responsibilities.
>
> New Forest owners are attempting to keep their animals in exactly the same way that owners of past generations have done. The problem is that there are now more ponies on less grazing.

Continuing its outright condemnation of the Forest's management, the BHS described worming provisions as 'totally inadequate' and made the point that 'the failure to wean foals results in mares attempting to support themselves, a yearling and a current or embryonic foal on what can best be described as a starvation diet from January to May every year'.

Harsh words, perhaps, but they highlight the unpleasant realities of ponies kept in the semi-wild state on ground that is incapable of supporting them and detract significantly from the traditional and very often romanticised ideal of the Forest and other moorland areas where the ponies help to project an altogether spurious image of rural life.

Before the ponies can be offered for sale they must be rounded up, tail-marked and branded. It is the job of the agisters to organise these 'pony drifts', which take place in September and October, but it is the mounted Commoners who provide the bone and sinew necessary for the job.

A 'pony drift', not unlike a Wild West roundup, is the most spectacular and exciting event of the New Forest year. It is rough, full-blooded and dangerous and definitely not for the unskilled or the faint-hearted. The ponies are driven into strategically placed wooden pounds, similar to those with which Western film buffs will be familiar. The intention is that they should be nudged forward at a steady pace, but good intentions rarely survive for long on the day of the pony drift, and once the herd is on the move galloping is the order of the day.

Many of the Commoners ride Foresters, often stallions, which are nimble, surefooted and can travel fast over the rough heather whilst displaying an uncanny ability to avoid the rabbit holes with which the rough ground is pock-marked. If the galloping herd gains the thick woodland cover and splits up, the task of rounding them up is made a hundred times more difficult and becomes, if anything, even more dangerous. Some of the pursuers put their trust, usually unwisely, in the bigger hunter type of animal, but it is rarely a match for the Forester on his own ground.

The drives, the hard riding, the wild yells and the spills and thrills of the chase last through the day and when the last drive is completed the colt-hunters dismount and with almost as much noise separate small groups of ponies and drive them into a much smaller enclosure, the crush. There, the agisters, apparently bearing charmed lives, get in amongst the squealing, steaming, milling ponies to tail-mark them by cutting the hair in a particular way, as proof that the owner has paid his dues for the year. Casualties among the colt-hunters are frequent and are regarded as an acceptable risk but agisters rarely, if ever, seem to sustain any injury. Thereafter, the foals that are to be left on the Forest are branded. This is man, or men, against a near-crazed animal and is in every way an elemental struggle. Surprisingly, it is accomplished without anyone being hurt.

Colt-hunting is a more specific exercise aimed at the capture of a designated animal or animals and it, too, is reminiscent of the Wild West show, the rodeo equivalent being, one supposes, the calf-wrestling event.

The hunters work in pairs over the rough ground, cutting out the required animal, which twists, turns and jinks whilst going as fast as it can lay legs to the ground. They ride alongside until they are close enough for one of them to seize the colt's tail. A quick, expert twist brings the pony down, the rider leaps from his horse to sit on the colt's head whilst the second horseman, having caught his companion's horse, gets a rope round the colt's neck. Then he secures it to one or other of the ridden horses so that the captive colt can be taken off to the pound.

The young and daring may employ an alternative method, the rider jumping at full gallop from his horse and pulling the colt down by getting his arms round its neck and wrestling it to the ground.

*New Forest Ponies in the natural surroundin*

*...at have influenced their development.*

# 5

# The Welsh Ponies

Of all the native breeds the Welsh is the most numerous. Supported by a strong and active breed society, Welsh ponies and cobs have been exported all over the world, and the USA, Australia, New Zealand and South Africa have their own Welsh breed societies, as do a number of European and Scandinavian countries.

Both the ponies and the cobs are bred extensively within the Principality and though they are no longer central to Welsh rural life they retain an appeal for Welshmen that has hardly been diluted by the advent of the tractor and the motor-car. The Royal Welsh Show is held annually at Builth Wells, near to the place where the last of the Welsh Princes of Wales, Llewellyn ap Gruffyd of Gwynedd, was killed on 11 December 1282 by the soldiers of Edward I, following his final, disastrous, battle against the English. For that reason Builth is enshrined for ever in Welsh history, but during the Royal Welsh week, when it becomes the focal centre for the Welsh breeds, history is made there again.

The number of entries is so great that the classes threaten to overflow the boundaries of the wide arena, and from early in the morning until late afternoon every seat in the huge grandstand is taken, whole families, sustained by sandwiches, cake and flasks of tea, watching every class throughout the day. Nor is this the sort of audience attracted to the run-of-the-mill county show: these are the *aficionados* and they are both knowledgeable and fiercely critical. Not for nothing is it said that every class at the Royal Welsh has a thousand judges!

Though they are the inheritors of a powerful Celtic horse culture the Welsh are not horsemen like the Irish and the Scots. Unlike those nations they have never had a cavalry regiment, for instance. But they are great stockmen and intuitive breeders and in that lies the strength of their ponies and cobs. They have, of course, the advantage of four distinct sections within the Welsh Stud Book. Two are for ponies and two for cobs, but at the base is the Welsh Mountain Pony which occupies Section A in the book and, with a height limit of 12 h.h. is the smallest of the four. From this foundation emanates the Section B Welsh Pony, height limit 13.2 h.h. and described as being 'more particularly – a riding pony'; and the two cob sections, C and D. Ideally, these last two should be no more than recognisably enlarged versions of the Welsh Mountain Pony.

The Welsh Pony and Cob Society Stud Book, opened in 1902 following the formation of the Society in the previous year, is obviously integral to the development of the Welsh breeds of ponies and cobs, and most particularly it marks the watershed between the 'old breed' and the new 'improved' modern ponies and cobs of a strictly fixed type.

Every breed society has an 'old breed' or type. It is, after all, a necessary part of evolution. (There is, for instance, no reason to suppose that there was not an Arabian horse of the 'old sort' hundreds of years ago in the evolution of that most ancient breed.) Without doubt, there was an 'old breed' of Welsh pony, though to give an exact definition of the type and any precise meaning to the phrase is now impossible. The interpretation depended upon the experience of individuals and the part of the country in which they lived.

In Wales, the development of the mountain stock was influenced significantly by the infusion of Eastern blood, a process that may have been started by the Romans and continued well into the nineteenth century by a number of Welsh landowners. As a result, the Mountain pony was lighter built and displayed a greater refinement, or quality, than did the heavier ponies used for shooting parties and harness work. These latter were more thickset and closer to the small Cob or, in modern parlance, 'the farm pony of Cob type'. In South Wales the coalfields of the Industrial Revolution encouraged the production of 'the pitter', which in some instances amounted to a powerful draught pony, not dissimilar from a miniature cart-horse and often displaying the plebeian attributes of a Roman nose and some heavy feather on the lower limbs.

The first Eastern influence on the indigenous Welsh stock was probably made during the Roman occupation of Britain. There were certainly plenty of ponies on the Welsh hills when Julius Caesar came to Britain in 55-54 BC and their use in chariots was well-established, Caesar himself writing of the Britons as being 'masters over their horses and chariots'. Almost certainly the Romans, who brought in Eastern-type horses, crossed those horses with the native stock. The Welsh Stud Book actually refers to the Romans as crossing the ponies

*Part of the famous Coed Coch herd of Welsh Mountain Ponies on the hills above Dolwen, N. Wal*

*Ponies on the Eppynt Hills, where Welsh stock has run since the time of the Romans.*

with 'Arabs'. In fact, the use of the word is erroneous: but the WSB is not alone in that, all too often in the history of every sort of equine there are these ambiguous references to 'Arab blood'. In fact, of course, there were no 'Arabs' as such at that time and there is no reason to suppose that there ever was a breed of horses native to Arabia as we know it. Certainly, neither the Romans, nor the Greeks before them, knew anything of an Arab horse and this infusion of Eastern blood to the Welsh breed was probably from a hot-blooded North African race or one from Western Asia: Persian, Libyan, Syrian or Barb. Nonetheless, whatever the origin, an Eastern influence was introduced nearly 2000 years ago and it was repeated through the subsequent centuries.

More indicative of the improvements made to the hill ponies by the great landowners of the Principality was the introduction of a Thoroughbred called Merlin, who was put out by the Wynn family on the Ruabon hills in the eighteenth century, probably as a result of an Act of 1740 which sought to exclude 'ponies' from the racecourse. This was some fifty years before the publication of *An Introduction to a General Stud Book* (1791) but by then the influence of the three founding fathers of the Thoroughbred, the Byerley Turk, and the Darley and Godolphin Arabians, was being felt increasingly. If the Act was the reason for the appearance of Merlin in North Wales then he would have been below 14.2 h.h., which was then the average height of the racehorse of the period.

Merlin was a direct descendant of the Darley Arabian and seems to have had no problems in withstanding the rigours of life on the hill. It would be unwise to attribute every significant improvement in the hill stock to this one horse but there is little doubt that he played a considerable part in its up-grading and was instrumental in providing a basis for the modern breeds. Today, the word 'merlin' has entered into the Welsh language, the word for pony being *merlyn*.

Half a century later Sir Robert Vaughan of Rug, Corwen, put out a part-bred stallion called Apricot on the hills around Merioneth. The Vaughans had imported what are referred to as Arab/Barbs, and Apricot was sired by one of these out of a Mountain mare. He won races all over North Wales and was just as hardy as Merlin, though this was not always the case when Eastern horses were put out to fend for themselves in an alien environment. A number were run out with native stock on the Brecon Beacons, in the Vale of Neath and elsewhere in South Wales, some of them it is recorded '... being quite incapable of enduring the hardships of the native mountain breeds'. Nonetheless, there was a notable refining influence as a result of these Arab and Barb stallions extending right into the nineteenth century and up to the arrival of the patriarch of the 'improved' Mountain

Pony, the legendary Dyoll Starlight (above), who not merely revolutionised the thinking of Welsh breeders by founding a new dynasty of beautiful ponies but was also responsible for the predominance of greys amongst the modern Section A stock.

Dyoll Starlight was by Dyoll Glassallt, a pony said to have been plain about the head but to have possessed exemplary limbs. Glassallt's distinctive feature was a large, white blaze covering much of the face. It still reappears in some of Starlight's many descendants and has become known as 'Glassallt's Badge'. Starlight's dam was Moonlight, described as 'a miniature Arab'. She was foaled in 1886 on the hills bordering Glamorgan and Brecon and was thought to be a descendant of the Crawshay Bailey Arab, a stallion put out on the Beacons in the mid-nineteenth century by the ironmaster of that name.

Starlight was bred in 1894 at the Glanyrannell Park Stud at Llanwrda, Carmarthenshire, owned by Howard Meuric Lloyd – the prefix Dyoll is Lloyd spelt backwards. Because of Starlight and his progeny the stronger, cobby sort of pony of the 'old breed' began to disappear, being replaced by an animal of far greater quality, freer moving and with the especially beautiful head which characterises the modern Welsh Mountain Pony.

Today, some sixty years after his death, the best Mountain Ponies and not a few of the leading Cobs trace descent from Starlight, and his blood remains unquestionably predominant in Australia, a country with a large and thriving population of Welsh stock. He was described by his breeder as 'the most beautiful pony in the whole world' – an assertion that has never been contested.

It was intended that when the doyen of the Welsh Mountain Pony reached the end of his life, having enjoyed his well-deserved retirement, his skeleton should be presented to the British Museum to honour his memory. Unhappily, Starlight died in a foreign land far from the rolling hills of Carmarthen and Meuric Lloyd's wishes could not be carried out.

Mr Lloyd, then suffering from a final illness, was persuaded by the acquisitive Lady Wentworth, daughter of Wilfrid and Lady Ann Blunt and the formidable owner of the famous Crabbet Arabian Stud, to sell Starlight to her. He did so, reluctantly, on the condition that the pony should never be sold and that his wishes regarding the skeleton should be observed.

Lady Wentworth reneged on the agreement and the whole affair became something of a *cause célèbre*. Finally after much prevarication and mounting pressure from Mr Lloyd's daughter and others she admitted in a letter to the magazine *Riding* that she had sold the pony to Spain in 1925 for £800 and that he had died there at the age of 31 in 1929.

The second of the 'improved' breed's great progenitors was Coed Coch Glyndwr, the foundation stallion of Miss Margaret Brodrick's Coed Coch Stud at Dolwen, situated in the hills behind Abergele, North Wales. Glyndwr through his sons and daughters, has to be seen as completing a metamorphosis between the 'old breed' and the modern, commercially viable, Welsh ponies. It is not an exaggeration to say that he changed for ever the course of Welsh breeding.

Miss Brodrick started her stud in 1924 and pioneered the promotion of Welsh breeds overseas. Her annual sales created a new dimension in the marketing of Welsh stock. On her death the stud was continued by her kinsman Lieutenant Colonel Edward Williams-Wynn, a member of one of the greatest of all Welsh land-owning families. It was dispersed in 1978 following the Colonel's death, but by then it had emerged as the most significant force ever in Welsh Pony breeding and the greatest single factor in the continuing evolution of the modern Section A and B ponies.

The world-wide influence of Coed Coch through two lifetimes was inestimable and it took place at a time that was most critical to the development of the Welsh breeds.

In the preface to Vol. 1 of the Welsh Pony and Cob Society Stud

Above: *The versatile Welsh Mountain Pony has always been a brilliant performer in harness.*

Below: *Nothing comes amiss to the Mountain Pony. This one, ridden side-saddle, is taking part in a musical ride.*

Book the following passage appears to emphasise the inter-
dependence of the Welsh breeds. Of the Stud Book it has this to say:
'It is not a jumble of all sorts and conditions of Cobs and Ponies in one
Stud Book but, as it were, a distinct Stud Book for each comprised in
one volume. Each variety is so dependent on, and is so closely
connected in its origin with the other, that breeders *will doubtless
from time to time take a dip into blood in one or other of the Sections
as may suit their purpose.*' (The italics are mine.) That statement
encapsulates the very essence of the Welsh breeds and is exemplified
in the pedigree of Coed Coch Glyndwr, a pony representing the near
perfect amalgam of Welsh bloods.

Glyndwr was by a pony of the previous generation, belonging to a
quite different era. He was Revolt, a red roan bred in 1909 by Miss
Eurgain Lort of Castellmai, Caernarfon. Revolt's dam was Llwyn
Flyaway, a daughter of the notable 14 h.h. Cob, Eiddwen Flyer, and
the lines were all to the great Cob sires, including one of the Cob
foundation stallions, Cymro Llwyd – and Cymro Llwyd was the
offspring of that Crawshay Bailey Arab!

Glyndwr's dam was Dinarth Henol – the name was originally
intended to be Gwenol, meaning 'swallow', but the handwriting of
her breeder, John Jones of Dinarth Hall, Colwyn Bay, was never the
most legible. She was a grand-daughter on her dam's side of Dyoll
Starlight, her sire being another of Marshall Dugdale's Llwyn Stud
ponies, Llwyn Satan. The most famous of Glyndwr's descendants
was his grandson Madog, close bred out of a Glyndwr daughter,
Mefusen, by his son Seryddwr. Madog became a sire of the calibre of
Starlight and Glyndwr and exerted a particular influence on the
Section C Pony of Cob Type through his son, the Palomino Lyn
Cwmcoed.

Even as we approach the twenty-first century the Welsh Mountain
Pony still reflects its early environment in terms of action,
conformation and constitutional hardiness. The conformation and
the action, although a product of environmental pressures, have been
refined and improved by human intervention and the employment of
selective breeding policies, as we have seen. The hardiness remains, or
should remain, unaltered despite the passing of many centuries.

The environment offered to the Welsh ponies was subject to the
harshest climatic conditions. The terrain was rough, marked with
steep inclines, strewn with boulders and shale and intersected with
deep and fast-flowing streams. Much of the upper ground was dotted
with treacherous bogs and many areas were impassable by any
means. The vegetation of these stark and wild uplands was sparse and
in winter, when the growth was cut back, much of it was covered in
frozen snow. The prime criterion for the Welsh Mountain Pony is

that it should be able to survive, and even thrive, in these conditions.

Against this background the ponies developed as small animals, offering a smaller surface area for the loss of body heat and requiring less food in order to maintain a viable condition. The shortage of food produced a remarkably efficient nutrient conversion ability in the ponies and to this day the Welsh breeds do best on a relatively restricted diet, something that is true of all the Mountain and Moorland breeds. Ponies moved to, or raised on, the lush southern pastures suffer as a result of an unaccustomedly rich food intake, becoming gross and highly susceptible to that crippling disease of the feet, laminitis.

Any move towards a significant increase in height in the Welsh pony breeds is likely to lead to a loss of type and character. Today, the conformation, despite the 'improvements' made by human intervention, still conforms to the terrain over which the pony had to operate. The feet, usually of dense, blue horn, are exceptionally hard. The cannon bones are short and strong and the body compact and notably deep through the girth. The Welsh talk about a pony having 'a good bread basket', and because of the depth of girth there is ample room for powerful lungs and a heart that is large in comparison to the overall size. The head, with small, pointed ears and dominated by a bold and very prominent eye, resembles, in part, that of the Arab, the nostrils in particular being large and open. The limbs are exemplary in terms of strength and conformation, the enormously powerful hindlegs and hock joints obtaining the maximum possible thrust because of their ability to be engaged well beneath the body. That movement is transmitted to the forelegs which are set a little back in respect of the relationship between the humerus and the scapula. In consequence, whilst the movement from the shoulders is free there is a definite knee action causing the foot to be lifted and then stretched forward before coming to the ground. This is the ideal action for an animal having to cross broken ground. Conversely, the long, low action of the Thoroughbred would be quite unsuitable for such conditions. The Mountain Pony and the Cobs all carry the light, silky feather at the heels which acts to drain off surplus water.

Constitutionally sound and hardy, the Mountain Pony has mental characteristics to match. He has a highly developed sense of self-preservation, an innate pony sagacity and an intelligence which allows him to learn quickly.

Quick and courageous, the Mountain Pony is a splendid child's riding and hunting pony and is a brilliant performer in harness, whilst as foundation stock for breeding bigger ponies and horses it is unsurpassed, although the full potential of Welsh and other native blood has yet to be realised.

In the past, when every homestead kept a pony or cob or both, the Mountain Pony was much used in harness as well as under saddle, and was quite capable of doing jobs round the farm. It could take produce to market, and up to the turn of the century, in North Wales particularly, ponies were even used to convey the dead over the mountain tracks from the hill farms to their resting place in the churchyard on the lower land. This service called for the use of two ponies and a hurdle with rough shafts at either end, the ponies being harnessed fore and aft whilst the coffin was secured in the centre. A hurdle of this sort can still be seen in the tiny Smugglers' Church on the seashore at Llanaber just north of Barmouth.

When Giraldus Cambrensis made his journeys through Wales in the last years of the twelfth century he found a fierce, warlike people much given to hunting, feasting and revelling. Inexorably that way of life was eroded by the incursions of the English kings, beginning with Edward I, and Wales did not find a new national identity until the Industrial Revolution of the nineteenth century and the spread of the Methodist chapels.

In the industrial south of Wales something of the old sporting traditions survived, as they do today when hunting is carried on enthusiastically by a dozen packs of hounds. In mid and North Wales, where the country was more mountainous, the chapel more restrictive and industrial development limited, the rural economy was backward and almost permanently depressed. In such a climate no sporting tradition was possible and to this day it would be a rarity to find a Gwynedd farmer, for instance, who had ever sat on a horse or indulged in field sports for pleasure. Nonetheless, neither chapel nor economic environment could prevail against the obstinate loyalty of the Welsh to the ponies of their land. They kept pony stock as a source of much-needed income and for their own utilitarian purposes, but they did so with great pride of possession, the pedigrees of the ponies often being recorded in the family Bible along with those of their owners. Their attachment persisted long after the tractor and the motor-car had taken over the work that had been done by the ponies, and today, throughout Wales, hill farms and smallholdings still carry a few head of ponies and some, of course, support more substantial herds. Many are carefully bred to the established lines and in the season their owners show them in-hand in competition with their peers at the numerous small country shows that command no more than a paragraph or two in the local paper and yet are of absorbing interest in the locality. The more committed and the more successful travel further afield to the larger border shows and, perhaps, go on to receive the supreme accolade, a rosette at the Royal of Wales.

Above: *Springbourne Caraway, a wonderfully correct example of the modern ('improved') Welsh Mountain* Pony. Below: *Revel Pavance in action. He is the senior stallion at Mr. and Mrs. Evans's Criccieth Stud, N. Wales.*

They finance their addiction by selling surplus stock at Gaerwen, Menai Bridge or Wrexham, or, for the better quality ponies, perhaps at the important Fayre Oaks or Royal Welsh sales, which attract buyers from England and almost as many from overseas.

At the bottom of the scale are the farmers working small acreages of marginal land who are to all intents and purposes no more than dealers in livestock. They too, however, maintain their links with the ponies. They buy the poorer stock at the smaller markets and they may breed a bit in haphazard fashion. Usually, their stock is moved on quickly to another market, the owners happy enough to take a few pounds profit from the meat buyers. Not surprisingly, they represent an ongoing animal welfare problem.

How well the Welsh breeders living in Wales market their product is arguable but about the quality of the product there can be no dispute. The ponies entered in Section B of the Welsh Pony and Cob Society Stud Book are probably possessed of a greater commercial potential in terms of performance but the best should be no less Welsh than their small Mountain compatriots.

There has been a Section B in the Stud Book ever since the publication of Vol.1 in 1902. It was devoted then, as it is now, to what the breed standard describes as 'a riding pony, with quality, riding action, adequate bone and substance, hardiness and constitution and with pony character'. The height limit for the Section is fixed at 13.2 h.h.

The modern, 'improved' Section B pony is certainly a riding pony of quality and it would be difficult to find anything so versatile in mainland Europe or elsewhere. By virtue of its size and action the Section B, with its well-proven jumping ability, has the edge on the Mountain Pony in terms of versatility and performance potential as well as its ability to carry older and bigger children. It has an exemplary riding action, too, low and economical with not much trace of the characteristic knee action of the Mountain Pony and the Cobs. On the other hand, there are those who hold that these refinements have been gained at the expense of the bone, substance and hardiness which are the essence of the Welsh breeds.

The early Section B ponies were often a cross between Mountain mares and small Cob stallions. They would carry a grown man shepherding on the hills and were once called the 'shepherd's pony'. They were more than capable of a day's hunting, too, and in North Wales these *merlins*, as they were known, rounded up ponies and the black, hill cattle in true Western style, the riders often carrying lassos like the American cowboy. Furthermore, they were hardy and well able to live out on the hill and fend for themselves which, as critics of the 'improved' type will argue, the modern pony would not.

This basic stock, like the Mountain Pony, was refined by the use of Arabs and small Thoroughbreds and also by 'Hackneys', although these latter would have been the old-fashioned all-round trotting roadster rather than the high-stepping harness horse of today's show-rings.

Without doubt the greatest influence in Section B breeding since the formation of the Stud Book was the famous Coed Coch Stud which, after Dyoll Starlight, had exerted a similar dominance over the Welsh Mountain through some memorable ponies.

It is generally accepted that the Welsh Pony, Section B, is founded on five principal sires and the pronounced Eastern influence is very apparent when these are examined individually.

The 'Abraham' of Section B, for instance, is Tan-y-Bwlch Berwyn, pictured below, (foaled in 1924) who was by Sahara, a Barb or more likely an Arab horse bought in Gibraltar in 1913 from a load of ponies brought there from Morocco. Put to Mrs Inge's Mountain mare, Brynhir Black Star, he sired Tan-y-Bwlch Berwyn. Mrs Inge owned the Tan-y-Bwlch estate at Maentwrog, Merionethshire, where she bred some excellent stock, being meticulous in her selection of breeding lines. Black Star, for instance, was the granddaughter of

Left: *A magnificent example of true Section B type, typifying the essential fire and presence of the Welsh pony.*

Right: *A Welsh Pony, the beau-ideal of the child's pony, at home in the hills of his native land.*

*Few ponies can match the dash, balance and agility of the Welsh Pony in gymkhana games.*

Dyoll Starlight through her sire, Bleddfa Shooting Star, and Dyoll Starlight's great-granddaughter on her dam's side.

During the Second World War Tan-y-Bwlch Berwyn went to Coed Coch where he bred Coed Coch Berwynfa out of his own daughter Berwyn Beauty who had a direct line through her dam to the Coed Coch's foundation stallion Glyndwr. Berwyn was one of the most successful of the famous Coed Coch stallions, each of which had a claim to fame in his own right, and he produced a whole generation of Coed Coch champions in both Sections A and B.

Less well-known is Craven Cyrus, founder of another early Section B strain. He is a further example of the Eastern influence and was a straight Arab/Welsh cross, his sire being the World Champion Skowronek (amongst the greatest Arabian sires ever) and his dam the Mountain Pony Irfon Lady Twilight, a Starlight daughter.

The second wave of Section B foundation sires is headed by Criban Victor, considered by many to be the archetypal Section B Welsh pony. Foaled in 1944 he was by Criban Winston, the son of Coed Coch Glyndwr, and his dam was Criban Whalebone by the Cob stallion Mathrafal Broadcast (14.3 h.h.), a horse regularly hunted by the Richards family of Criban, the oldest of the Welsh studs.

Reeves Golden Lustre had a strong Arab connection on the side of his dam, though his sire Ceulan Revoke was a Glyndwr grandson.

Solway Master Bronze, the last of the founding stallions, retired in 1974 after siring 541 foals. He combined the best blood of Coed Coch and Criban for he was by Glyndwr out of Criban Biddy Bronze.

After these predominant sires the most important is Downland Chevalier (foaled 1962). He grew over height to 13.3 h.h. but he headed the sire ratings between 1973-80 and must be regarded as being a major factor in the modern Welsh Pony.

Welsh Ponies are in demand all over the world as competition and show ponies, for which role they are ideally suited. However, they are also much used in harness, in which occupation they excel like all the Welsh Cobs and Ponies, and they form a large percentage of the entry for the popular and well-filled working hunter pony classes and are not out of place in a pure show class.

The advantage of the Welsh Pony as an all-round performer suitable for the most ambitious child is that unlike the Riding Pony and some of the Thoroughbred crosses it retains its native character. It is in most instances hardy, inherently sound and is economical and easy to keep — a big consideration when children are at school and ponies have to be looked after by Mother. Temperamentally it is sensible, good-natured and intelligent but it has courage and great competitive ability on account of its conformation and natural athleticism.

# 6

# *The Welsh Cobs*

The highlight of all classes at the Royal Welsh Show is the day when the main ring is dominated by the Welsh Cobs. At no other show in Britain, or perhaps in the whole world, does a single breed, shown in hand, inspire such enthusiasm or generate such open and highly vocal partisanship. The Cobs, it is said, are as integral to whole sections of Welsh life as the Nonconformist chapel, the male voice choirs and rugby football at Cardiff Arms Park.

The climax of the day comes when the Cobs are run out by their shirt-sleeved, plimsoll-shod handlers. No pin-stripe suits and bowler hats here as in the English rings, and indeed there will often be a team of two or three running a single Cob in relays. This is the moment when the continual rumble of sound in the stands and at the ringside erupts into roars of appreciation and encouragement which are surely heard over the border in England, thirty miles away.

It is, of course, enormously exciting to see these charismatic cobs powering over the grass, driven by the enormous, propulsive force of the hindlegs, their handlers at full stretch. Indeed, the Welsh have a word which exactly embraces the heightened, charged atmosphere created by the 'running of the Cobs'. The word is *hwyl* and there is no exact English translation: the nearest would be 'fervour', of the kind associated with religious intensity. Even the uninvolved onlooker is hard put to resist being caught up in the excitement of the moment, but it is possible that the pounding, heavily-shod hooves, the flashing plimsolls, the sharp cries of encouragement are hardly conducive to the making of an objective assessment of the Welsh Cob.

Nor is that assisted by the use of heavy shoes on feet that are allowed to grow longer than usual. The result is to produce an exaggerated lift in the high knee action which has no appeal for the breeders of hunters and competition horses. In fact, when the feet are trimmed normally the action allows the Cob to cover a lot of ground

*Nebo Bouncer, Welsh Pony of Cob type (Section C)*
*was bred in Cardigan at the Jones Family's Nebo Stud.*

at each stride. The knee action, of course, remains naturally high but the leg, following the lift, is then extended fully to the front before being put to the ground.

The pure-bred Cob, either Section D, which may be of any height but is often between 14.2-15.2 h.h., or the smaller Welsh Pony of Cob Type, Section C in the Stud Book, which does not exceed 13.2 h.h., are enormously effective performers in harness and are also, within their limitations, excellent saddle horses. One would not choose a pure-bred Cob to go hunting in Leicestershire, but there is no better choice in a tight, hilly country where speed is not of the essence. The Cob is strong enough to carry any weight, it is infinitely enduring, it has the courage of a Thoroughbred, it jumps carefully and very well, having an innate sense of self-preservation, and it is extraordinarily sure-footed, hence its typical lift of the knee to avoid stumbling on rough ground. Moreover, it is sound to the nth degree and easily kept, for it thrives on minimal rations. Indeed, for the Welsh Cob as for its pony brethren, lush grazing and indulgent feeding are contrary to the natural metabolism and constitute a recipe for disaster.

If the Cob is crossed with a Thoroughbred the accepted practice is to put 'blood on the top', but there is a school of thought that would reverse that precept and put the Cob stallion to the Thoroughbred mare so as to preserve more of the Cob character. The result in either case is a 'competition horse' insofar as dressage, showjumping and hunting are concerned. The second cross to the Thoroughbred produces the event horse, giving the progeny greater scope, speed and a somewhat lower, longer action whilst retaining some of the sense and a lot of the constitutional soundness.

One particular conformational asset in the Cobs, as in the Mountain Pony, is the possession of exceptionally good hocks of enormous strength. The hock is the hardest worked joint in the equine frame and it is in consequence subject to various disorders that can lead to unsoundness. In the Welsh breeds the hock is nearly always in exact alignment with the other components of a near-perfectly proportioned hindleg. No uneven wear is therefore possible. Furthermore, the hock itself is a large joint, as big and usually bigger than that in much larger animals, but never round or fleshy. It is capable of maximum flexion and thus contributes materially to the tremendous propulsive force of the quarters and hindlegs. Curbs, that is strains of the ligament joining the hock to the cannon bone and seen as a thickening immediately below and round the point of the hock, rarely occur in the Welsh breeds any more than do disabling spavins, the inflammation of bones in the joint which leads to loss of flexion and lameness.

The hereditary attributes of a strong constitution and soundness of wind and limb; the stamina and powers of endurance; the predominant courage; the ability to thrive at a minimal subsistence level, together with the 'street wise' character of the Welsh Cob, are derived from the Welsh Mountain Pony, which is the foundation for all Sections of the Welsh Stud Book. These ponies we know benefited from infusions of Eastern blood brought to Wales by the Romans, but there is much evidence of a Spanish influence, too, in the development of both the Section C and D Cobs. Spanish horses in considerable numbers were present in Wales during the twelfth century, and Giraldus Cambrensis, Archdeacon of Brecon and historian of mediaeval Wales, records the presence of studs of Spanish horses in Powys, south of Bala. His descriptions of the horses he encountered in his journeys through Wales are comprehensive and carefully considered and it would seem that most of the animals he saw were not unlike the present-day Welsh Cob. Of the breeding of those horses he wrote that there were ' . . . most excellent studs put apart for breeding and deriving their origin from some fine Spanish horses which Robert de Belesine, Count of Shrewsbury, brought into this country: on which account the horses sent from hence are remarkable for their majestic proportion and fleetness'.

The Section C Cob, not incorporated into the Stud Book until 1949, can be assumed to have resulted from a crossing of Mountain mares with the naturally smaller cobs which were always in evidence and were in effect larger, more thick-set versions of the Mountain Pony. The most significant Section C Cob stallions of recent years are Synod William and Lyn Cwmcoed, pictured opposite, both of whom have a strong Welsh Mountain Pony background, their sires being Section A stallions of the famous Coed Coch lineage.

Whereas in the Mountain Pony breeding areas Cobs inclined more to pony character, in Cardiganshire, the heartland and spiritual home of Cob breeding, and in Carmarthenshire and Pembroke, the type was far stronger built, showing the influence of the now extinct Welsh Cart-horse, a compact, slightly bigger version of the Cob which had evolved as a result of the occasional infusion of heavy horse blood.

The forerunner of the Section D Cob was the Powys Cob, the product of the crossing of the indigenous stock with the Spanish imports. It was to be the principal remount of the English armies from the twelfth century onwards.

The present-day Cobs owe much to the later influence of Norfolk Trotters or Roadsters and the Yorkshire Coach Horse (basically a Thoroughbred/Cleveland cross).

The four horses regarded as 'foundation' sires for the modern Cob and appearing most frequently in Stud Book pedigrees are:

Trotting Comet, foaled in 1840 out of a famous Cardiganshire trotting mare by Flyer, a blind black horse whose sire was a Welsh Cart-horse and whose dam was of English (probably Norfolk) trotting blood.

True Briton, foaled in 1830, was by the Yorkshire Coach Horse Ruler, out of Douse, reputedly an Arab but described as being all Welsh Cob in appearance.

Cymro Llwyd, foaled 1850, was a dun or perhaps a Palomino. He was by the Crawshay Bailey Arab, a horse put out on Brecon Beacons by the ironmaster Crawshay Bailey whose family were to become the Lords of Glanusk. He was out of a Welsh trotting mare and is largely responsible for today's duns, creams and Palominos. His most famous descendant was Llanarth Braint who had no less than thirteen crosses to Cymro Llwyd in his pedigree.

(The Llanarth Stud founded in 1936 did more than any other to popularise the Welsh Cob as a riding horse and to promote

*The late Viscountess Chetwynd's Lyn Cwmcoed*

*A Section C Cob under saddle. They jump well and are wonderful hunting ponies for children.*

*The champion Welsh Cob stallion Derwen Replica bred by Mr. and Mrs. I.J.R. Lloyd at their International Welsh Cob Centre in Dyfed.*

*Llanarth Flying Comet, one of the all-time greats in the cob world, takes time off in his paddock.*

Cob sales overseas. Llanarth was founded at Blaenwern by the late Pauline Taylor and Barbara Saunders-Davis, whose place in the partnership was later taken by Enid Lewis, a professor of music in London. The two 'ladies of Blaenwern' were then joined by Len Bigley, who showed the Llanarth Cobs with great success and now continues to breed the Llanarth lines at his own stud in Hereford.)

Alonzo the Brave, foaled in 1866, stood almost 16 h.h. and was a perfect example of the Norfolk Roadster, although he is often, in accordance with the usage of the time, referred to as a Hackney. His ancestry traced to the Darley Arabian, one of the founding sires of the Thoroughbred, through the great Norfolk Shales horses; Shales Original and Norfolk Shales, and thence through Sampson, Blaze and Flying Childers, the first great racehorse who was the son of the Darley. On his dam's side his ancestors included the Derby winner Emilius.

In Wales Welsh Cobs were used for every sort of farm and harness work almost up to the Second World War and many, including the smaller Section C Cobs, were and still are hunted on the hills by full-grown men. In this last context the smaller Cob remains a wonderful hunting pony for both young people and light adults and is much in demand for driving turnouts.

Between the wars Section D Cobs were supplied in large numbers to the Army as draught horses and as troopers for mounted infantry, and there was also a huge trade in Cobs from both sections of the Stud Book with the big city dairy companies, bakeries and so on.

Before the introduction of stallion licensing in 1918, Welsh breeders practised their own form of 'performance testing', selecting breeding stock on the basis of trotting matches or tests. Many of them were two-horse, spur-of-the-minute races from the market, often that held at Llanybyther, down the Cardigan lanes to the homestead. In the south there was a favourite route from Cardiff to Dowlais. It was 35 miles, uphill all the way, and a good Cob covered it in under three hours.

Above: *The Royal Welsh showground at Builth Wells during the judging of Welsh Cobs, classes which are integral to the show.* Left: *The essence of the unique Welsh Cob movement is characterised by* the propulsive thrust of the quarters.

Below: By Appointment – a royal carriage drawn by a pair of Welsh Cobs against the backcloth of Windsor Castle.

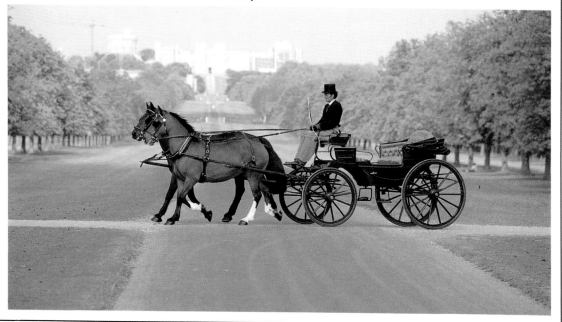

# 7

# *The Dales and Fell Ponies*

Geographically, the difference between the Dales and Fell Pony is customarily defined as being east and west of the Pennine range respectively. The Dales belong to the Upper Dales of Tyne, Allen, Wear and Tees in north Yorkshire, Northumberland and Durham, whilst the Fell occupies the northern edges of the Pennines and the moorlands of Westmorland and Cumberland.

Genetically, the early origins of these two northern breeds bear an even closer relationship. Both, long ago, derived from one type or another of the indigenous British pony. Later, during the Roman occupation, there is evidence of the black Friesian horse influence, which is still apparent.

In the pattern of equine breeding the Friesland is notably under-rated. Bred on the sea-girt land of Friesland in the north of the Netherlands, it is a cold-blood with roots going back to the primitive Forest Horse of Europe. Tacitus (AD 55-120) records its existence and acknowledges both its antiquity and its value as an all-round work-horse. About the Friesland's appearance he was less complimentary, remarking on the animal's exceptional ugliness.

Nonetheless, 1000 years later the relatively small Friesian, which was no more than 15 h.h., carried the Friesian knights and their German neighbours to the Crusades, and though not in the class of the Andalucian and the purpose-bred horses of Lombardy, was recognised as the most practical war-horse of Europe, con-stitutionally hardy, up to weight and the cheapest to keep. Much later, in the seventeenth century, use was made of the Friesian in the breeding of the Württemberger at Marbach, the court stud of the Dukes of Württemberg since the sixteenth century and the oldest of the present German state studs, and the impressive carriage horses of the Oldenburg breed were also founded largely on Friesian blood.

Its contribution to the British breeds, particularly to the Dales and

Fells which still resemble it closely, began long before that when the Roman Legions were stationed in the northern counties as a deterrent to the marauding Picts. Rome, following its usual practice of employing auxiliaries and later federates as the flank-guard for the Legions, used troops from Friesland. The Friesians were seafarers as well as agriculturalists. As traders they favoured a roomy type of merchant ship, big enough for the transport of livestock, and in these they came to Britain bringing with them their black horses. Sixteen centuries ago a cohort of Friesian horse was stationed at the Roman fort of Rudchester on Hadrian's Wall and later larger detachments were deployed further to the west around Carlisle.

Many of these Friesian horsemen and their horses chose to stay, and their settlements are commemorated in names of villages and towns all over the eastern part of Britain. Friston and Frisby are examples, the names meaning 'settlement of the Friesians'; whilst in Cumbria there is Frisington 'the village of the sons of the Friesians'.

After the fall of the Roman Empire in the West the native Friesians developed a thriving seaborne trade in livestock, horses, cloth and swords, using Dorestad as their commercial base. Some time after AD 800 Dorestad fell to the raiding Norsemen, but by then the Friesian horse was well established in the great central valley of Norway, Gudbrandsdal, which gave its name to a race of horses now more usually termed Døle Gudbrandsdal, and the breed maintained a

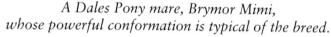

*A Dales Pony mare, Brymor Mimi,*
*whose powerful conformation is typical of the breed.*

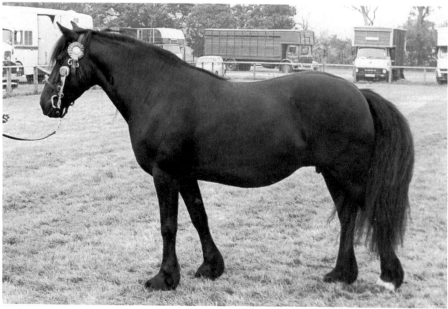

Above: *A Dales mare with foal at foot engaged in the traditional role of shepherding on the upland pastures.*
Below: *Although heavily built this Dales mare, and her attractive foal, move with* *great activity and freedom.*
Right: *There could be no better way of seeing the Pennine country than from the back of a tireless Dales Pony.*

considerable presence on both sides of the British Pennines. Fifteen hundred years later, there is still a distinct resemblance between the Norwegian horse and the Dales and Fells, visual as well as historical evidence of a common root in the Friesian horse.

A later, refining influence, extending well into the eighteenth century and beyond, which was instrumental in forming the character and increased activity of the two northern breeds, was the strong, swift-running Galloway which, particularly in the case of the Fell Pony, represents a distinctive presence. It can, indeed, be regarded as the link between the Highland Pony, of the old, lighter Island type, and the ponies of the northern fell and dale country. The Galloway was bred in the area between Nithsdale and the Mull of Galloway and it was the mount of the old border raiders and then of the Scottish drovers bringing cattle over the Pennine tracks. It stood between 13-14 h.h., was infinitely enduring and was noted for its sure-footedness in rough country and for its remarkable speed either under saddle or in harness. As a breed the Galloway ceased to exist before the end of the nineteenth century but not before it had left its mark on the northern breeds and had even played a not inconsiderable part in the evolution of the English Thoroughbred as part of the 'running horse' stock which provided the foundation for the Oriental out-crosses of the seventeenth and eighteenth centuries. Until quite recent times both Dale and Fell Ponies were often termed 'Gallowa' in popular speech, the name being applied loosely to anything under 15 h.h.

Inevitably there was also considerable cross-breeding between the ponies of the dales and fells. Two of the six Fell premium stallions selected in 1912 by the Board of Agriculture, Dalesman and Highland Fashion, were by Yorkshire Fashion, a black horse of 15 h.h. described in the Fell section of the Polo and Riding Pony Society stud book as a 'pure Dales Cob' and as being by a 'Norfolk Cob'. It was not until 1924 that Dalesman was re-registered as a Dales Pony.

The distinction in size, proportion and appearance between the Dales and Fell Ponies of today, however, is due largely to functional rather than geographical reasons.

The Dales Ponies worked underground in the lead mines of Allendale and Alston Moor once horizontal levels were introduced there in the nineteenth century and they carried the lead ore, after it had been washed, down to the seaports of the Tyne. They were also employed in coal-mines and as general carriers, capable of hauling loads quite out of proportion to their size. They worked in pack trains, under loads of up to 2 cwt. borne in panniers, and as general utility animals for farm-work. Above all, the old-time Dales Pony was a great and fast trotter, able to cover a mile in three minutes

*A champion Fell Pony mare, Lownthwaite Rossetta. Although lighter than the Dale the resemblance is evident.*

carrying considerable weight. Welsh Cob blood was introduced to the breed in the nineteenth century, in particular that of the trotting stallion Comet, and there was also a considerable Clydesdale infusion. Indeed, when the Dales Improvement Society was founded at Hexham in December 1916 one of its concerns was to discourage the Clydesdale cross.

Writing in 1917 F. Garnett, then the secretary of the Fell Pony Committee, commented that, 'The Dales are, with very few exceptions, two-thirds Clydesdale and have gone on the heavy side as far as the Polo pony has gone on the blood side.' He also remarked on the excellence of the Dales' bone, legs and feet, considering the breed as being, 'for Army purposes, second to none in the Country'.

The present-day Dales Pony still has wonderful bone and limb as well as the characteristic hard, blue feet. It retains its great strength and weight-carrying capacity and whilst it is a heavier animal than the Fell, its relationship to the Clydesdale is hardly apparent. It remains a brilliant, courageous performer in harness and is used increasingly under saddle. Its temperament, frugality and soundness of constitution make it a particularly good choice for trekking activities. Predominantly black in colour, although there are also bays, browns and some greys (a legacy, perhaps, of the Clydesdale), it stands up to 14.2 h.h.

Above: *A group of exceptional Fell ponies in the natural setting provided by the Cumbrian fells.* Right: *As befits the descendant of the old swift-running* Galloways, the Fell is remarkably handy under saddle. Below: *H.R.H. Prince Philip driving his team of Fell Ponies at the Harrods' Driving Grand Prix at Windsor.*

The Fell Pony, also at one time called a Brough Hill Pony on account of the Brough Hill Fair where many came up for sale and where pony racing once took place, was in its time as notable a pack pony as the Dales, and upon the Fell pack trains depended the Kendal wool and cloth trade to far-off Southampton in the sixteenth century. The Fell ponies were also notable trotters, as they are still, and were used in harness, on the farm, and under saddle for herding and droving. Indeed, the Fell enthusiasts will hold that the pony is primarily of saddle type despite its success as a driving pony. Certainly, the modern Fell, 'constitutionally as hard as iron' as the breed standard has it, is a very good riding pony in its own right and an excellent cross to produce small hunters and riding horses. Lighter-built than the Dale, it stands at 14 h.h., the accepted colours being black, brown, bay and grey.

Perhaps the most famous of the early Fell stallions, whose name also figures in Dales breeding, was the eighteenth-century Lingcropper, responsible for the strain bearing his name. He was found during the Jacobite rising of '45 on Stainmore, Westmorland, 'cropping the ling' and still carrying his saddle, his rider having, presumably, been killed. It is likely that he was a Galloway.

This stallion founded a strain of exceptional ponies including Lingcropper Again, foaled in 1900, and the late Roy Charlton's Linnel Lingcropper. The Charltons and their Linnel Stud were the major influence on the Fell pony in the twentieth century and are still in the forefront of Fell breeding today. At the turn of the century Roy B. Charlton was producing 14 h.h. ponies that would carry a rider of 15 stone (210lbs) and mature years comfortably, safely and with acceptable expedition, and their descendants are still able to do so. The Linnel Stud pioneered the export of ponies abroad, selling to countries as diverse as India, Spain and South America, and produced generations of show-ring winners.

In the late nineteenth century Christopher Wilson of Kirkby Lonsdale created the Hackney Pony by using local Fell Pony stock as the foundation and adding to it some Welsh pony blood from North Wales as well as that of the Norfolk Trotter.

At the turn of the century both Dales and Fells (the latter then categorised with the Dales) were still running wild on the hillsides in small herds and breeding naturally. That is no longer the case, but whilst both breeds are now bred in various parts of the country, the centres of breeding remain in the north of England where the breed shows are held.

The Dales, a breed considerably less numerous than the Fell, have a breed show at Barnard Castle, whilst the Fell show is at Penrith later in the year during October.

# 8

# *The Highland Pony*

It seems certain that there were indigenous ponies in the northern parts of Scotland and the islands following the Ice Age. The suggestion has been made that this was Pony Type 2 resembling the Asiatic Wild Horse, with a possible cross with Pony Type 1 which became the Celtic Pony. Thereafter, during the Bronze Age, there is archaeological evidence of horses being brought in from Scandinavia and later from Iceland. Today there are definite resemblances in the Highland to Nordic horses like the Northland, Güdbrandsdal and the Norwegian Fjord.

All these breeds have ancient origins and, indeed, the famous cave drawings at Lascaux in France, thought to be 15-20,000 years old, depict horses that are surprisingly close in conformation and colour, particularly the variations of dun, to the modern Highland. Dun, in all its shades, is the colour of the 'primitives' and is almost always accompanied by a dorsal 'eel' stripe and sometimes by barred or 'zebra' leg markings as in the Lascaux paintings. Today's Highlands include all shades of dun with an eel stripe, whilst the zebra markings are by no means uncommon. Other colours found in the Highland are grey, brown, black, occasionally bay and sometimes a spectacular bloodstone chestnut with silver mane and tail.

Much use has been made of outcrosses in the development of the modern Highland. Around the year 1535 the size and quality of indigenous stock was much improved by French horses, which would certainly have included what we would now call Percherons.

Spanish horses were being used for the same purpose in the seventeenth and eighteenth centuries. Both the islands of Rhum and Mull benefited, it is thought, from horses shipwrecked in the area following the defeat of the Armada, but that and any possible long-lasting effect is open to doubt, as are all the other stories of shipwrecked Spanish horses altering the course of a breed's

Above: *The 'primitive' dun colouring and the accompanying dorsal eel stripe is a characteristic of the Highland.*

Left: *A traditional use for the Highland was the carrying of the heavy deer carcasses from the hill.*

Right: *The Highland, much used in the trekking industry, is a good all-round riding pony.*

*This striking study of a Highland mare belonging to H.M. The Queen shows off the powerful build.*

development. However, there is indisputable record of the Uist stock being improved by Spanish horses brought back from Spain by the Chief of Clanranald just prior to his death at the Battle of Sheriffmuir in the first Jacobite rising of 1715. The odd Dale and Fell pony was also introduced as well as at least one Hackney-type pony, which would have been of the old trotting Roadster sort. (The Hackney descends from the Norfolk Roadster and the word at that time described an active riding horse used specifically for road journeys.) This latter was brought to the Isles in 1870 and was a notable influence on the Arran ponies.

As is often the case in the upgrading of breeds, it was Oriental blood, either Arab or Barb, which had the greatest effect. The Dukes of Atholl, who bred Highlands extensively and selectively for centuries and whose stock became a cornerstone for the breed, were using such horses in the sixteenth century. The famous Calgary strain of Highland evolved by J.H. Monroe-Mackenzie has at its base the Arab horse, Syrian. Monroe-Mackenzie moved to Mull in 1886 to manage the Calgary Estate and used the Arab 'to get better backs and shoulders on the Highland ponies'. In fact Syrian, when put to the smaller island ponies, produced offspring which were too small, but he was far more successful when used on the bigger Mainland ponies. The fillies produced in this way were put back to the famous Highland stallion Isleman (foaled in 1893) and the subsequent progeny established the very distinctive Calgary type.

Arabs were also imported by the Macneils of Barra and they too produced a particular stamp of pony, small, not more than 13 h.h. refined in appearance and with an Arab-like head. They were light and active with a reputation for speed and stamina.

Until relatively recent times there were undoubtedly two types of Highland pony, that bred on the Western Isles and the bigger, more powerfully built Mainland pony. The pony of the Western Isles was of riding type, though also used in harness and on the land. The stronger Mainland was closer to a draught type but he too was also ridden. A common and much misused name for the Mainland pony was Garron, which, in fact, means no more than gelding. In time the division betwen the types disappeared and today no distinction is made between the two.

The Highland pony of whatever type was the original all-purpose horse of the Highlands and Islands of Scotland. It provided the only means of locomotion other than by foot and it was invaluable on the crofts for every kind of farm work, being used as a pack horse as well as in draught. It was easily kept and thrived on rough pasture. It was inherently sound of constitution, strong, sure-footed to a degree and

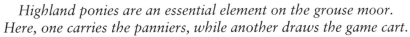

*Highland ponies are an essential element on the grouse moor.*
*Here, one carries the panniers, while another draws the game cart.*

*The Highland is capable of every sort of work and is us*

*timber hauling on H.M. The Queen's Balmoral estate.*

remarkably docile. Today, there are few ponies who exhibit such an in-bred ability to get over very rough boggy land as the Highland.

Traditionally, the Highland pony was also used on the hill to carry game panniers, as a riding pony, and also for carrying deer carcasses, which may weigh up to eighteen stone (252lbs). The strength of the breed, combined with an uncanny surefootedness and a sensible, unflappable temperament make them particularly suitable for this latter task for there are very few equines which will carry a dead animal with equanimity. Because of this equable temperament it is sometimes thought that the Highland is a dull lack-lustre creature, but nothing could be further from the truth. The Highland is a sensitive animal and very responsive, with a great capacity for affection.

What is perhaps not so generally appreciated is that the Highland ponies, which had always had a military role, continued to be used in that capacity up to the turn of the century. In fact, the South African War, in which the Lovat Scouts were mounted on Highlands, encouraged Highland pony breeding when it was at a low ebb. Another Scottish regiment raised by the Marquis of Tullibardine, Tullibardine's Scottish Horse, also went to war on Highland ponies and the Atholl ponies were certainly present at Edinburgh in 1903 as part of the Scottish Horse complement.

Although the Dukes of Atholl had bred ponies for centuries their first recorded stallion was Morelle foaled in 1853 and he was a piebald. His son, Glen Tilt and his grandson Glengarry I were both significant in the breed's development but the greatest name of all was that of Herd Laddie who became a veritable partriarch of the breed.

Herd Laddie's most famous sons were Bonnie Laddie, still considered to have been the best type of Highland ever, and Glenbruar who was responsible for much of the success of the Rosehaugh stud. Glenbruar sired the best-known Highland of all, Jock, born in 1921 out of Lady Strathnairn. This grey pony achieved fame as the favourite mount of King George V who 'took him to Balmoral and Sandringham and never rode any other pony when he was out shooting. He was a perfect pony in every way. . . . ' So wrote the Crown Equerry, Sir Arthur Erskine, who had bought Jock from Major Logan of Inverness.

The Highland Pony, with a breed height limit of 14.2 h.h., is amongst the largest of the native ponies and is certainly as strong as any of them. This height, however, is of relatively recent origin and may be due largely to the influence exerted by the Department of Agriculture for Scotland, which before 1924 operated studs on Skye and at Faille and then at Beechwood, near Inverness. The demands made by forestry in Scotland for heavier animals able to put more weight into the collar for tree haulage encouraged the Board to produce bigger ponies up to 14.2 h.h., and to this end it is probable that Clydesdale blood was introduced. Otherwise much smaller ponies unaffected by this infusion lived on islands such as Barra during the last century.

The modern Highland is an ideal family pony. It is by no means fast but it is a willing jumper and makes a good, safe and economical hunter in enclosed or rough countries. The Thoroughbred/Highland cross, with perhaps a return to the Thoroughbred in the next generation, makes a very good hunter or competition horse which frequently retains the hardiness and good sense of the Mountain and Moorland connection. Highlands still work in forestry and on the hill carting deer, and they are still used on small farms, but because of their strength and good temperament they are also in much demand as trekking ponies. Trekking, indeed, is virtually a Scottish invention. It was pioneered by the Ormiston family in the early 1950s and it was Ewan Ormiston who coined the name pony-trekking, the word trekking (i.e. going on from place to place) being, it is said, brought back from South Africa with the Lovat Scouts. Many hundreds of Highlands are now involved in what has become something of a boom industry and there is no doubt that trekking has been a major factor in the encouragement of breeding.

*The Countess of Swinton's mare Laura of Dykes,*
*Champion Highland, Royal Show 1983.*

*Shetland Grand Nationals, in aid of charities, are a popular and exciting show-ring attraction.*

# 9

# *The Shetland*

The Shetland Pony, whose original habitat is the Shetland Islands lying some hundred miles north of Scotland, is the smallest of the British pony breeds and in proportion to its diminutive size is probably one of the most powerful equines in the world with the possible exception of the mule. The Shetland Pony Stud Book Society was formed in 1890 and is the oldest of all the pony breed societies. It lays down in its official standard an average height of forty inches at the wither, the Shetland being measured in inches rather than in the customary mediaeval measurement of hands, that is the four inches which was taken as being the measurement across the back of a man's hand. Maurice Cox, the breed's accepted authority, however, wrote in *The Shetland Pony* that he considered '38 inches is the height which will be found to lend itself best to symmetry and activity, while retaining the individual character of the breed'.

The base foundation colour of the breed is black, but brown, chestnut and grey are also found, and the Shetland Society, alone amongst the breed organisations, also accepts skewbalds and piebalds.

The Shetland is probably the purest of the native breeds, largely because of the isolation of its geographical position. The harsh environment of the Islands, the severe winter weather and the paucity of sustaining forage, governed the character and small stature of the ponies, and gave them their ability to survive and even thrive on minimal feed. Even when raised away from the stark Island conditions the size of the Shetland remains unaffected, although better keep greatly increases the risk of laminitis unless proper management is practised.

It is not possible to establish definitely the early origins of the Shetland prior to the Bronze Age, but there is likely to have been a connection between the ponies of Tundra type and the Scandinavian stock. The Tundra is the obscure fourth primitive whose remains, along with those of the mammoths, have been discovered in north-east Siberia, where winter temperatures are below those at the North Pole. Also concerned would have been the smaller 'mountain' type pony from southern Europe standing at about 12 h.h., perhaps a hand less than the Tundra. These ponies could have crossed from Iberia over the grasslands then covering the continental shelf without difficulty.

Later, during the second and third centuries AD, ponies which would have been exposed to an 'Oriental' influence were certainly brought in from the Celtic settlements. After them came the Vikings, who settled in the northern isles and brought their 'horses' with them in their longboats. Ornamental stones found on Bressay and Burra in the Shetlands are dated to about the end of the ninth century AD and show men mounted on small, light-boned, active ponies which, in comparison with the human figures, could not have exceeded forty inches.

The Shetland's relationship to the primitive Tundra and the breed's area of origin in the northern latitudes is emphasised by their peculiarly large nasal cavities. These cavities are necessary to warm the freezingly cold air before it enters the lungs and they are not found in equines originating in warm climates.

On the Islands the ponies were used for every sort of work on the crofts and as pack animals for the carrying of seaweed and fetching ('flitting') peat for winter firing. The lairds used the Shetland to pull small gigs and the like and it could easily carry a grown man over rough going.

Otherwise, Shetlands were exported from the Islands for all sorts of purposes. Apart from their use as children's ponies and in harness, they appeared in circuses and exhibitions and were kept as an attraction in public parks and in the grounds of great houses. In 1815 the Marquis of Bristol kept a herd of Shetlands in the park at Ickworth, Suffolk.

The Act of 1847 which prohibited the employment of women and children in coal-mines, where their job was to haul the coal-tubs, often on hands and knees because of the low roofs of the tunnels, created a new and for a time a seemingly insatiable demand for the Shetland. Eventually, to meet the requirements of the pit-trade, a thicker, heavier pony evolved, coarser in the head, longer and with a straighter shoulder. In 1915 Professor Bryner Jones wrote, 'There are two types amongst Shetlands, one with a coarse head and collar fitting, rather than saddle shoulders; and the other with smart blood-like head and riding shoulders.'

There were efforts to introduce outcrosses to the Islands but they

*Show classes for Shetlands, like this prize-winning mare,*
*are held at major shows.*

made no impression on the native stock and are certainly not apparent today. The most notable were the Arab taken to Fetlar in 1837 by Sir Arthur Nicholson and more recently a Highland put there unwisely by the Department of Agriculture. There were also Norwegian ponies put out on the Sumburgh estates.

A significant date in the history of the Shetland is 1870 when the Marquis of Londonderry formed his stud at Bressay. Much of the top quality Shetland stock can be traced back to the famous Londonderry sires, in particular to Jack and his sons Lord of the Isles (exported to America on the stud's dispersal in 1899), Laird of Noss and Odin.

Today, the Shetland, now consistent enough in type, is bred in large numbers in mainland Britain. In addition stock is still maintained in the original habitat, and the fact that the standard of Island stock has so much improved was the result of the work done by Mr and Mrs Maurice Cox in the introduction of premium schemes, inspection and so on.

The Shetland has been described as 'a cart-horse in miniature', which is quite incorrect. It is rather a pony of excellent proportions, strongly built with the best of limbs, a neat head, broad across the forehead, and at its best it exhibits a free, dead straight action. Shetlands are shown extensively in-hand, in harness and under saddle, too, the standard of exhibits being generally high in respect of conformation and action.

Left: *The little mare Doodle is a Shetland character. She is seen here in the Christmas pageant at Olympia.*

Opposite: *Doodle in retirement on Shetland. During her working life she raised large sums for the children's hospital at Great Ormond Street.*

Below: *Shetland ponies thrive on sparse grazing. Their metabolism is not suited to lush pasture.*

Below right: *Bincombe Venture in the snow. This outstanding stallion was virtually unbeaten in a brilliant show-ring career.*

The breed has been exported all over the world and it is probably true to say that the pure Island stock is no longer a significant factor in Shetland breeding. The first export, of 75 ponies, was made to Eli Elliot in America in 1885 and an American Shetland Pony Club was formed three years later. Canada was also a good market and so was Australia, where the true Shetland is still bred. In Europe Holland is the biggest market and may, indeed, by now have more Shetlands than Britain. France, Sweden and Belgium, as well as Holland, have their own stud books.

The Shetland, as we have seen, does not take to crossing, but the Americans and Canadians have succeeded in producing their own distinctive types, in particular the American Shetland, a smart harness pony which, it has to be said, bears little resemblance to the original Shetland of the Islands. It is claimed that the 'new breed' retains the native hardiness, constitution and frugality but that is unlikely and will in any event never be put to the test.

The 'breeds' produced on the Shetland are the American Shetland (an amalgam of Hackney blood topped up with some Arab and small Thoroughbred); the Pony of the Americas (which began when a Shetland stallion was put to an Appaloosa mare) and, in South America, the pygmy Falabella.

In fact, both the American Shetland and the Pony of the Americas have by now emerged as distinct types in their own right. The former is ridden and jumped as well as being raced in harness and shown in the ring as a harness pony. The Pony of the Americas is now to all intents a pony version of the popular Appaloosa horse.

In recent years there has been a movement towards the breeding of novelty 'miniatures' in Europe, the Shetland stock being bred down by selectively mating the smallest specimens.

# 10

# *The Connemara*

The Irish pony which we call Connemara takes its name from that part of Ireland to the west of Loughs Corrib and Mask, a region bounded on the south by Galway Bay and facing the Atlantic Ocean on the west. This wild, empty land of bogs, lakes and mountains is the natural habitat of the breed, the ponies subsisting on the rough herbage available in conditions of considerable severity.

There are, however, compensating factors which have contributed to the development of the breed as well as to Ireland's reputation as a country particularly suited to the raising of horses. The west of Ireland is as wet as anywhere in Europe, but it is warmed by the Gulf Stream, and that combination of wet and warmth result in a long season of plant growth. The Atlantic coastline is certainly subject to the most ferocious gales, but frosts are unusual and only the highest land is affected by snow.

The ponies feed on coarse grass, herbs, reeds and gorse, all of which sprout early in the year and are still in growth well into the winter. The soil will often be thin, but it is nonetheless rich in phosphates and minerals and many of the ponies are able to supplement their diet with iron-rich seaweed, as do some of the Shetlands bred on the Isles. The southern part of Connemara is rockier than the rest and the land is much poorer. Ponies reared there are, in consequence, smaller – no bigger than about 13 h.h. – than those bred on the better lands which may grow up to a height of 14 h.h., the upper limit set by the Connemara Pony Breeders' Society of Ireland.

The modern Connemara relies upon a mongrel background more than some of the other native breeds. A variety of bloods have been concerned with its evolution but, for all that, its natural environment remains probably the greatest factor in the formation of its particular and special character.

*The Connemara in its native habitat on t.*

*ugh moorland bounding Galway Bay, Ireland.*

Predictably, the origins of the Connemara are by no means clearly defined. It is, without doubt, the sole 'indigenous' equine of Ireland, and before the Celtic incursions along the west coast in the fifth and sixth centuries BC it would not have been dissimilar to the ponies which had inhabited Shetland, Norway and Iceland from the times of pre-history.

The Celts, with their distinctive horse culture were, in time, to become the pre-eminent traders in the area, and were responsible for the first introduction of an Eastern influence to the indigenous pony population. From the beginnings of their settlement the Brigantes of Ireland maintained a connection with their compatriots in Spain, and it is Spain, along with Morocco and then Arabia itself, which is the key to the development of the Connemara pony. There is constant evidence of the import of Spanish horses, which were recognised throughout Europe as being far and away superior to any others from the time of the Celts onwards.

When Galway City was in the heyday of its prosperity during the sixteenth century the wealthy merchants there, who carried on a thriving trade with Spain, imported Andalucian horses which were said to be the best that money could buy. Mention is also made in City records of Spanish Barbs, which were probably much the same thing, for the Andalucian derives much of its character from the Moroccan Barb.

More Spanish horses are believed to have entered Ireland as survivors of those extraordinarily numerous vessels of the Spanish Armada supposedly wrecked along the Irish coast. The inflated numbers excepted, it is not improbable, but the significance of their effect upon the equine population can hardly be regarded as a major factor in the development of the Connemara.

All these crosses produced the renowned Irish Hobby of the sixteenth and seventeenth centuries, which was so much in demand for military as well as civilian use. This hardy, agile pony, often possessed of the ambling or pacing gait, later played a part, like the Galloway, in the evolution of the English Thoroughbred when it was crossed with imported Eastern (Arabian) stallions. The Hobby was described by Richard Berenger, Gentleman of the Horse to George III, as possessing 'a fine head and strong neck, a well-cast body, strong limbs, sure of foot and nimble in dangerous places, of lively courage and tough in travel'.

Arab blood was brought into Connemara by some of the nineteenth-century landowners, notably the Martin family, to which belonged both 'Humanity' Martin, founder of the Society for the Prevention of Cruelty to Animals and Violet Francis Martin (Martin Ross), the sporting novelist. In the latter part of the century Welsh

Cobs were also used under government horse-breeding schemes in an effort to halt the decline in the Connemara stock caused by the impoverished state of the Irish agricultural community. One of them was Prince Llewellyn whose son Dynamite, out of a native mare, was the sire of the famous Cannon Ball, the first stallion to be entered in the first Connemara Stud Book.

The subsequent Royal Commission of 1897 appointed to examine horse-breeding in Ireland was headed by Professor J. Cossar Ewart of Edinburgh, a man whose contribution to equine development and study has yet to be exceeded. It is not too much to claim that it was Ewart's Commission which laid the foundations for the modern Connemara.

Ewart himself wrote of the old dun type of Connemara as being 'capable of living where all but wild ponies would starve'. They were, he continued, 'strong and hardy as mules, and so fertile and free from hereditary diseases that their extinction would be a national loss . . . I was struck with their strength, endurance and easy paces . . . with their intelligence and docility and with the capacity for work under conditions which would speedily prove disastrous to horses reared under less natural conditions'. One distinguished witness to give evidence before the Commission, Samuel Usher Roberts CB, declared that the ponies were 'without exception the best animals I ever knew . . . an extremely hard, wiry type of pony showing a great deal of the Barb and/or Arab blood'. Lord Arthur Cecil, a notable authority,

*A near-perfect example of the modern*
*English-bred Connemara, the mare Rosenharley Rossleague.*

Above: *In its native land the Connemara is used for every sort of light farm work.* Left: *The Connemara, with its free movement and natural jumping ability, is* an ideal competition pony. Below: *The level-headed Connemara performs as well in harness as under saddle. The dun colouring is characteristic of the breed.*

commented on the good riding shoulders and 'a marked natural proclivity for jumping', and the latter remains the hallmark of the modern Connemara.

The Commission advised the use of Thoroughbred, Roadster and Hackney blood (the last two not being all that dissimilar at that period). Very much less desirable was the introduction of a Clydesdale cross, though fortunately this was no more than a temporary aberration.

A Connemara Pony Breeders' Society was formed in 1923, the year after the attainment of Home Rule in Ireland. The first Stud Book, in which 75 mares and six stallions were listed as being of suitable type, was published in 1926.

Rebel, foaled in 1922, and Golden Gleam, born a decade later, are both recognised as playing a major part in the Connemara development, but one should not forget the grandson of the Welsh Cob Prince Llewellyn, the grey Cannon Ball, who was born in 1904 and who despite his Welsh blood was as Irish as they come. He was a very great sire, but he also had the distinction of winning the Farmers' Race at Oughterard sixteen years in succession, being fed half a barrel of oats the night before the race! Frequently, he trotted home from market on his own, his owner, Harry Toole, lying dead drunk in the well of the cart. When he died a wake was held for him which lasted right through the night and into most of the following day.

Recent lines are those of Carna Dun, by the Thoroughbred Little Heaven, who sired the famous showjumper Dundrum, and there is also that of the grey Thoroughbred, Winter. There are two particularly notable Irish Draught sires, Mayboy and Skibbereen; there is a continuing Welsh connection through Dynamite, who appears in the fifth Stud Book (1943), and an important line through Clonkeehan Auratum (1954-76). He was by the justly famous pure-bred Arab, Naseel, founder of a dynasty of British Riding Ponies.

If this all seems to be something of a melting pot, one must remember that it is not unusual or inadvisable to introduce outside stallions of a *fixed* breed so as to retain and ensure the required type. In this case the proof of the pudding is in the eating. The result is a brilliant performance pony in its own right: fast, courageous, level-headed and a superb jumper. When crossed with the Thoroughbred the Connemara produces as good cross-country horses as any in the world, horses that still retain much of the inherited native qualities of soundness and constitutional hardiness derived from the wild environment.

Connemaras are universally of the best riding type, and they are quality ponies which can also be used in harness. In England, where the ponies grow bigger, the English Connemara Pony Society (formed in 1947) sets a height limit of 14.2 h.h. which confers greater scope and makes the pony suitable for adults as well as children.

Connemaras, almost without exception, exhibit elegance combined with substance, they are beautifully proportioned with good fronts and have an exemplary length of rein, that is the length from poll to wither along the top of the neck. As a special bonus they have the best bone for their size in the business – an astonishing 7-8 inches below the knee. The movement is free with not much trace of knee action and, of course, they have an exceptional, almost inbred, jumping ability. Colours are grey, which is probably the most common, black, bay, brown and dun.

Connemaras are in great demand throughout Europe, and countries like Germany breed and sell large numbers, the ponies being put through rigorous performance and selection tests. In Ireland Connemaras are still plentiful in their original habitat and the Society carries out careful inspections of young stock in the early summer followed in August by the annual breed show at Clifden. A number of animals are sold at Clifden but the principal sale of Irish Connemara stock is at Maam Cross in October, an event attended by a number of overseas buyers.

# 11

# *The Cleveland Bay*

From mediaeval times a strong bay-coloured pack-horse was bred in the north-east quarter of Yorkshire's North Riding, an area which includes Cleveland. North of the Tees this clean-legged horse was called a Vardy – interestingly, *vardo* is the Romany word for a gypsy wagon – whilst in the South it became known as the Chapman Horse because of its use by the chapmen who were the merchants, travelling salesmen and carriers of the day.

A Chapman Horse would carry a pack-load of about two hundredweights, twice the 'seam' able to be packed by any other breed, and it was used extensively to carry to the sea the ironstone, potash and alum from the mines that were a major industry of Cleveland from Roman times.

The Chapman was by no means so impressively proportioned as the modern Cleveland and, indeed, it was probably not much bigger than the present day Dales Pony. However, it had clean legs – that is, no feather on the lower limbs – and it must have had exceptional strength in the back and loins, although that part would have had more length to it than we are accustomed to see and perhaps find acceptable today. For a pack horse, however, a longer than usual back is a necessity if it is to be able to carry a big load comfortably, whilst clean legs were just as essential in the deep Cleveland clay.

The Chapman was undoubtedly a versatile horse. It worked on the land, went in harness, and it carried the farmer and his wife to market, she riding pillion behind her husband with the farm produce stowed in panniers around her. On Sundays the same horse took the family to church, the children taking up the space previously occupied by butter, poultry and cheeses.

It was from this horse that the Cleveland Bay derived, though exactly how is by no means certain. Without doubt there was in the latter part of the seventeenth century a considerable number of

*Clevelands have been in regular use at the Royal Mews for two hundred years.*

Andalucian (Spanish) stallions in the North-East of England, a legacy of the Civil War and its aftermath. The Andalucian horse of the time was the war-horse *par excellence*, the equivalent of the modern general's staff car, and there were certainly a number of redundant chargers in the area following the Restoration. It is reasonable to suppose that such horses played a significant role in the evolution of the Cleveland Bay, which today still displays characteristics reminiscent of the Andalucian, particularly about the head. The other influence has to be that of the Barb, for there was constant trafficking between the Barbary Coast and the north-eastern sea towns on account of the harbour works at Tangier which were carried out by Yorkshire contractors after Catherine of Braganza brought the port to the British crown on her marriage to Charles II.

What is certain is that recourse was never made to cart-blood from the heavy breed of the day, the Old English Black. Nor was there Thoroughbred blood as we know it – indeed, that word in the early eighteenth century had yet to be coined. 'No taint of Black nor Blood' was always the proud boast of the Cleveland breeder.

However, two notable sires do appear in the early history of the Cleveland which are entered in the *General Stud Book*, Vol. 1, published in 1808 following preliminary editions and the initial appearance in 1791 of *An Introduction to a General Stud Book*. These were Jalap by Regulus, the son of the Godolphin Arabian out of Red Rose, and Manica, foaled in Yorkshire in 1707 by the Darley Arabian out of Darley's Jester. Their blood was maintained in the Cleveland breed principally through Sportsman 299 (foaled in 1876) and Barnaby 21 (foaled in 1860). Three other noted foundation sires of the eighteenth century were Dart, Barley Harvest and The Hob Hill Horse. They appear, however, without benefit of pedigree, which is not to say that their breeding was unknown but only that as they came from the area it was probably never thought necessary to commit it to paper.

Otherwise there is no evidence of outside influences, and by the end of the eighteenth century the breed was pronouncedly fixed in type and as unmistakable as it is today.

A typical Cleveland Bay stands between 16-16.2 h.h. and is a powerful, very active, clean-legged horse with, says the breed standard, '9 inches or more of good, flat bone below the knee'. The colour is always bay with strong black points. White markings, beyond a small star, are not acceptable. When mature, which is not until six or seven years of age, a Cleveland measures as much, if not more, from wither to elbow as from elbow to the ground. It is a long-living breed and a very fertile one, whilst for generations a natural jumping ability has been a notable feature.

The Cleveland Bay was the only horse able to work the heavy clay lands of the North-East and because clay is by nature holding, those clean legs were an essential attribute. It hauled heavy loads in testing conditions; it carried big men to hounds and was in no way deterred by being asked to jump out of deep clay, and it was also a powerful coach horse, unsurpassed by any other, at least up to the end of the eighteenth century.

With the advent of the new macadamised turnpikes speed became of the essence and the Cleveland was deemed too slow for coaches scheduled to average 8-10 m.p.h. As a result a new breed evolved based on the Cleveland. This was the Yorkshire Coach Horse, a Thoroughbred/Cleveland cross or, more usually, the product of a half-bred Cleveland stallion out of a Cleveland mare. A Yorkshire Coach Horse Stud Book was formed in 1887, four years after the establishment of the Cleveland Bay Society which published its first Stud Book in the following year, its first editor being William Scarth Dixon, the leading hunting, racing and agricultural correspondent of the day who was also the Society's first secretary. The purity of the breed was preserved by enforcing the old policy of 'neither Black nor Blood'. The Coach Horse Stud Book remained in being right up to 1936 when the breed in respect of a 'closed' stud book had to all intents disappeared.

*A fine example of the Cleveland Bay,*
*the ideal cross to produce competition stock.*

During the nineteenth century the Cleveland Bay, like its Andalucian forebear two hundred years previously, became a significant up-grading force throughout Europe and was exported as far afield as South Africa, India, Russia and America, where a breed society was formed in 1889. The Electoral Studs at Celle, in Hanover, and at Oldenburg had made extensive use of the Cleveland in the latter half of the eighteenth century and, indeed, Champion (54), exported to Germany in the 1850s, was being used at Hanover up to his death at the age of 28 years.

The decline of the Cleveland Bay only began after the First World War, and this process was accelerated after the Second World War. By 1962 there were only four mature stallions left in Britain and that the breed survived at all was largely due to the intervention of HM The Queen, who bought a colt that had been destined to go to America. This was Mulgrave Supreme, bred at Duell's Dale House, Staithes, one of the oldest established of the great Cleveland studs. He became a wonderfully successful sire and within fifteen years the number of stallions in Britain had increased to 36, many of which were the progeny of this prepotent horse.

The Cleveland Bay has, in fact, enjoyed Royal support for some two hundred years. George II was an enthusiast for the breed and the Queen's grandfather, George V, was also a keen supporter. In Vol. XVI of the Stud Book he is shown as the owner or breeder of no less than 26 horses in the part-bred Register and five pure-breds in the main Stud Book. Although Cleveland Bays have always featured at the Royal Mews the breed was given additional encouragement by the Duke of Edinburgh's successes with them in competition driving and the enthusiastic support of Colonel Sir John Miller, Crown Equerry from 1961-87.

There are still uses for the pure-bred Cleveland but the breed's greatest asset is its prepotency when crossed with other breeds, to which it transmits size, bone, constitutional hardness and usually jumping ability. A first cross produces middle- and heavyweight hunters with a talent for jumping, and excellent brood mares, which when put back to the Thoroughbred produce the faster horse needed for cross-country competition. Prepotency in the breed is assured in a manner denied to the Irish Draught, for instance, and most of the remaining European warm-bloods, which are inevitably of a genetically mixed background. The Cleveland Stud Book closed in 1883 and since then there has been no outside blood introduced to the breed. It follows, therefore, that if a stallion meets the requirements of conformation and movement its prepotency will be assured.

Furthermore, the cross to the Thoroughbred is a natural one and its success understandable because of the close association of the breeds.

Above: *Cleveland Bay stock in their traditional surroundings in the north-east of Yorkshire's North Riding.*

Below: *A Cleveland Bay, saddled for a postillion, in preparation for a State occasion.*

The Thoroughbred foundation mares of the late seventeenth and early eighteenth centuries were almost all resident in the Vale of Bedale, next door to the Vale of Cleveland and there has to be an influence on the Cleveland on that account. No Thoroughbred horse foaled after 1820 appears in the Cleveland Bay Stud Books but the few recorded before that date carried the very best distance blood (that is, over four miles) of the eighteenth and early nineteenth centuries. There exists, therefore, a special compatibility between the two breeds, the pure, prepotent Cleveland blood compensating for any of the Thoroughbred failings.

The cross has produced numerous international showjumpers – Harvey Smith's Madison Time and the Barkers' North Flight are two examples – as well as event horses like the Canadian Sumatra and Rembrandt and dressage performers of the quality of Lady Joicey's Powder Monkey.

Nonetheless, there is cause for concern and disquiet about the breed's future. The danger in using a breed extensively as a base stock for crossing is that it is possible to overlook the fact that the future lies in the maintenance of a national *pure-bred* herd to provide that crossing base. At the present time the shortage of pure-bred fillies is serious and if the trend continues could be disastrous for one of Britain's oldest breeds.

*Storth House Temptation by Knaresborough Warlock, winner of the Cleveland Bay class at the Great Yorkshire Show 1981.*

# 12

# *The Irish Draught*

It is acknowledged that some of the best cross-country horses in the world are bred in Ireland, and that the foundation of those celebrated Irish hunters is the 'horse of the countryside' which has become known as the Irish Draught.

Without doubt, there is the influence of that ubiquitous Spanish horse on earlier indigenous stock, but the size and character of the breed would have come from the Great Horses, mostly northern French and Flemish, which were brought into Ireland from the time of the Anglo-Norman invasion of 1172. The Flemish or Flanders Horse, now called the Belgian Heavy Draught or the Brabant, after one of the principal breeding areas, was famous throughout Europe in the Middle Ages and had a great effect upon the breeding of the war-horse. It was instrumental to a large degree in the evolution of the English Great Horse and later in the development of its successor, the Shire. Centuries later it provided a base for the Clydesdale and it even had a considerable effect upon the Suffolk Punch. These strong Flemish and related French mares when crossed with imported Eastern and Andalucian horses in time resulted in the Draught horses which were used for every sort of purpose in harness and under saddle on the small Irish farms, the mares being bred from each year.

By 1850 the Irish Draught was described by contemporary observers examining the agricultural situation following the 1847 Famine as being a low-built animal not exceeding 15.2-3 h.h., with much bone and substance, the body being set on short, strong, clean legs. The back was short, the loin strong, but the quarters were inclined to droop and goose-rumps were prevalent. The horse was generally somewhat upright in the shoulder, though the neck was strong and the head small. The action, allowing for the slope of the shoulders, was straight and level, though not extravagant. These animals could trot in harness and could canter and gallop under

Above: *A champion Irish Draught mare, typical of the sort which produces the top-class Irish hunter.*

Below: *The Irish Draught is a performance horse, athletic and with natural jumping ability.*

*Blue Henry's head reflects the good sense and bold outlook of the Irish Draught horse.*

saddle well enough. Furthermore they were reputed to be excellent, careful jumpers. This last sterling quality arose out of the Irishman's love of hunting and his natural ability to ride young horses across a country in a snaffle bridle and with the aid of an ash-plant. It was customary for Irish horses to be both lunged and long-reined over banks, whilst foals and yearlings called into a yard made their way there over any obstacles that happened to be in their path, as many still do to this day.

It all resulted in horses which developed an innate talent for finding their way over the most fearsome of obstacles and it survives in the present day Irish stock. The rich limestone pastures and the wet, mild climate, which give a long growing season, produced bone, substance and size in the Irish Draught, whilst the Thoroughbred cross gave quality, scope and greater speed without detracting from the inherited hunting sagacity.

After the Irish Famine of 1847 the number of Draughts declined and efforts were later made to improve the remaining stock with Clydesdale and some Shire crosses. These were not successful and had a coarsening influence. The Clydesdale is also held responsible for the breed becoming somewhat tied-in below the knee, a fault which it has taken a long time to eradicate. (The term tied-in is used when the measurement below the knee is less than that taken above the fetlock joint. The construction restricts the passage of the tendons and indicates insufficient bone to support the body weight without risk of damage to the limb.) Thomas Meleady, giving evidence before Professor Ewart's Royal Commission of 1897, spoke bitterly of the

*The famous and very successful Irish Draught stallion, Enniskean Pride.*

effect of 'the Scotch horses' on the Irish stock. He called them 'heavy-legged horses, easily tired' and claimed that it was the Clydesdale which destroyed the Co. Mayo pony stock and that of Wicklow and Wexford as well.

The breed was much improved by the stallion subsidies made available in 1904 by the Department of Agriculture Committee on Horsebreeding. Fortunately, Ireland, unlike England, has always recognised its horses as a national asset and encouraged their breeding and sale accordingly. In 1917 a *Book for Horses of the Irish Draught Type* (not a Stud Book but rather a register since there were no recorded pedigrees) was introduced in which 375 mares and 44 stallions were entered as being sound and suitable.

Up to the beginning of the Second World War a good trade for the breed was enjoyed for use as vanners, army remounts and draught horses and, of course, as a base for the celebrated half-bred hunter. Inevitably the war brought about a decline in standards, though since then there has been a revival in the fortunes of the Irish Draught.

In 1976 the Irish Draught Society was formed to promote and preserve the breed and three years later the Irish Draught Horse Society (GB) was formed in England and within a very short period of time became one of the most progressive of British horse societies. It operates a grading system to produce in due course animals that can be registered as Irish Draught, and its influence on hunter breeding has been remarkable, many show-ring winners of recent years being either by or out of Irish Draughts. The national mare band is still worryingly small in numbers, but the choice of top-class Irish Draught stallions in Britain is wide. Used on Thoroughbred mares the Draught stallions pass on bone, substance, size and usually their jumping ability, too. Moreover the Irish Draughts and their progeny are easily managed. They are rarely sick or sorry and they thrive on smaller, plainer rations than other breeds of comparable size.

The modern Irish Draught is bigger than its predecessors of a century ago, and most of them now stand at 16 h.h. with the stallions often reaching 17 h.h. The quarters and the set of the tail are much improved and there is little evidence of being tied-in below the knee in today's stock. They retain the massive limb and bone but most of them are extraordinarily athletic – many of the stallions standing in Britain are regularly ridden, hunted and jumped and plans are in hand for the introduction of performance testing.

The Irish Draught is a good riding horse in its own right, as Mr Keith Luxford's famous pure-bred champion show cob, Grandstand, showed. However, the great value of the breed is as a foundation for the production of sound three-quarter, or seven-eighths bred horses as well as middle- and heavyweight hunters.

The world-famous Whitbread Shires at work in the City of London, where until 1991 they were a popular sight.

# 13

# *The Shire Horse*

The massive, majestically moving Shire Horse, standing over 17 h.h. and weighing more than a tonne, is bred principally in the Fen country and the counties of Leicester, Stafford and Derby. It descends from the English Great Horse of the Middle Ages, which in turn was derived from those heavy horses brought into England after the Norman Conquest, themselves descendants of the primitive European cold-blood, the heavy Forest Horse referred to in Chapter 1. However, just how 'great' was the Great Horse is not perhaps generally appreciated. From the evidence of sixteenth-century horse armour that can be seen at the Tower of London it seems that the Great Horse was, in fact, a heavy type of cob that was not more than 15.2 h.h. and bore little resemblance to the massive modern Shire.

Essentially it was the end of the sixteenth century which marked the appearance of the heavy draught horse in Britain. The Great Horse, no longer needed to carry the heavily armoured horsemen of a previous era, was being put to hauling the heavy wagons and coaches of the period across the countryside. 'Hauling' is the appropriate word, for the roadways were no more than rough tracks, horrendously rutted in the dry summer weather and deep in mud during winter.

Writing of the importation of heavy horses during this time, Thomas Blundeville, author of *The Four Chief Offices of Horsemanship* (1570), mentions specifically the German draught horse, the Almaine, the Friesian and the Flemish or Flanders horse. Without any doubt it is this last horse, like the Friesian predominantly black in colour, which had the greatest influence on the evolution of the British Shire. Again and again this large, slow-moving, heavy animal, bred on marshlands not unlike those which supported its far-off ancestor the Forest Horse, appears in the development of the Shire and it is generally regarded as the principal ancestor of the breed. Nonetheless, the more active Friesian also played an important part, the cross introducing a refining element and a better, freer movement. The German horses mentioned by Blundeville do not appear to have had any lasting or noticeable influence.

The biggest single factor in the breed's development occurred in the first half of the seventeenth century when work began on the draining of the Fens. The Dutch contractors imported their own Flemish horses, for the work was demanding of both strength and weight. These horses stayed on to breed and they and their progeny thrived mightily on the rich lands created by their labours.

It is at this point that we hear no more of the Great Horse, the English draught horses from the Midland counties taking on the name of English Blacks, or Old English Blacks, a name, incidentally, bestowed by Oliver Cromwell, himself a Huntingdon man and a noted agriculturalist. In fact it is more likely that the future Lord Protector was referring to Friesian horses but the name stuck and passed into general usage.

The Old English Blacks lived on into the Restoration and in the reign of Charles II the King's Household Cavalry were mounted exclusively on them. To this day, the Life Guards and the Blues and Royals use black horses obtained largely in the Midlands and a bit further to the north of England. In a sense the black horses of Charles's Household Cavalry were a relic of the war-horse of the Middle Ages which they closely resembled. By no means speedy, they were nonetheless showy enough for ceremonial purposes and, very importantly, they were cheap to keep!

The honour of being recognised as the Shire breed's 'foundation' stallion belongs to the Packington Blind Horse who stood at Packington near Ashby de la Zouche between 1755 and 1770. A black horse, he appears in the first Shire Stud Book because of the number of horses claiming descent from him.

The first Stud Book was published in 1878, two years after the formation of the English Cart Horse Society which had the patronage of the Prince of Wales, a royal association which was to continue up to our own time. In 1884, after much contention, the Cart Horse Society changed its name to the Shire Horse Society, by which title it has been known ever since.

Between 1901-1914 over 5000 animals were registered each year and breeders enjoyed a thriving export market to the USA. After the Second World War, however, there was little place for the Shire either in industry or agriculture and numbers dropped. The great brewing companies, however, remained loyal users of the breed and the subsequent revival in the fortunes of the Shire owes much to their support, and perhaps something also to the evergreen Drive of the Heavy Horses at London's Horse of the Year Show at Wembley. Today the annual Shire Horse Show at Peterborough attracts over three hundred entries and upwards of 15,000 enthusiastic spectators.

The modern Shire, with greater quality than his forebears, inclines more towards the type that developed in the Midlands than the coarser Fen strains. The bone of the Shire, that is the measurement below the knee, is expected to measure 11 inches and whilst the legs carry considerable 'feather' it is fine and silky, quite unlike the heavy coarse feather which was commonplace half a century ago and which at one time did the breed no good in the American market. The most popular colour for the Shire is still black with white feathering, although there are numerous grey teams to be seen. Bay and brown are also acceptable.

The enormous strength of the docile Shire can be gauged from a glance at just a few of the weight-pulling records. In 1924 at the Wembley Exhibition, for instance, a pair pulling against a dynometer (a device for measuring mechanical power) exceeded the maximum possible reading. It was estimated that they exerted a pull equal to a starting load of fifty tonnes. The same pair, driven tandem and working on slippery granite setts, shifted an actual load of 18.5 tonnes, the shaft horse starting the load before his leader had got into his collar.

Although it is not always appreciated as being stock suitable for crossing, Shire crosses with the Thoroughbred are on the increase. The progeny on the first, but more particularly the second, cross are big, heavyweight hunter types of bone and substance. Furthermore, they seem to retain the quiet temperament of the Shire. They may not be the fastest of horses but they are powerful and well-suited for either dressage or showjumping. Assurance, one of the best show heavyweight hunters of the 1980s, had a background of Shire blood and 25 years ago a number of Britain's top international jumpers were part-bred to Shire horses.

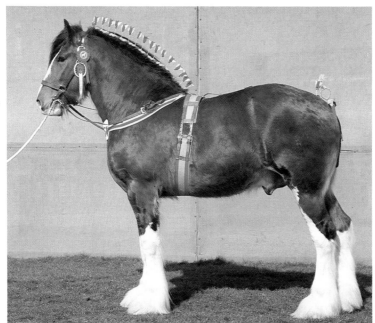

Left: *The modern Shire, standing over 17 h.h. and weighing a tonne, has greater quality than his forebears.*

Right: *A huge entry of Shire turnouts at the popular breed show held at Peterborough and the champion's lap of honour in front of the crowded grandstand there.*

Below: *The Whitbread Shires, used regularly for beer deliveries until recently, were housed in upper-floor stables in the centre of London.*

# 14

# *The Suffolk Punch*

The dictionary definition of the word 'Punch' is endearing – 'a variety of English horse, short-legged and barrel-bodied, a short, fat fellow' – and it describes its subject admirably.

The Suffolk Punch is the oldest of Britain's heavy breeds and quite the most unmistakable in appearance. William Camden, writing in his book *Britannia* (1586), refers to the Suffolk breed as having been established some eighty years previously. Nonetheless, the early origins remain obscure, possibly because of the insular independence of the East Anglian character. Time and again in breeding records there is reference to 'a mare' or 'So-and-so's mare' and even to 'So-and-so's Old Horse'. Even the pedigree of the first great racehorse, Flying Childers, shows the grand-dam as 'mare'. It was not that the details were unknown. Indeed, it was just the opposite: they were so well-known throughout the Eastern Counties that it was not felt necessary to record them, and so far as the strangers outside East Anglia were concerned it was none of their business.

Yet it was in East Anglia that so many of the most famous horses in Britain were bred; horses that were to be of great and lasting influence far beyond the counties' borders. Most notable were the great trotting Roadsters of Norfolk and this tradition of trotting horses in East Anglia is first made evident in the Domesday Book of 1085 where a large proportion of Norfolk manors are shown as possessing substantial numbers of *runcini*, the strong Rouncys which were in later times described as being 'hard trotting cobs'.

The Roadsters, operating in both Norfolk and Suffolk and beyond carried the posts long before the post-chaise and John Palmer's mail coaches, the first of which made the run from Bristol to London on 2 August, 1784. Carrying a man of average size, say twelve stone (168 lbs) or thereabouts, they covered the ground at speeds of up to fifteen to sixteen miles to the hour. Trotting matches were a common feature in the life of English sporting society in the eighteenth century and the early years of the nineteenth, and the records are impressive. The celebrated trotting mare Phenomena, as a twelve-year-old, went seventeen miles in 56 minutes on the Huntingdon Road and later improved on that performance by covering the distance in under 53 minutes. Bellfounder, who went to America in 1822 to play a part in the evolution of that country's Standardbred, the world's supreme harness-racer, was able to trot two miles in six minutes and nine in under half an hour.

All this trotting blood, founded on what Thomas Blundeville of Norfolk referred to as 'our mares' and what in the language of Gervase Markham, a Nottinghamshire man, were called 'plane breede English hors both syre and damme', was interwoven with coaching blood in the form of the Yorkshire Coach Horse, and with that of the early Arabian sires and their derivative which became known as the Thoroughbred. It would be incomprehensible if these Roadsters, many of them sorrel or red roan in colour, did not play their part in the evolution of the Suffolk Punch along with the heavier Flanders mares, which, of course, were also good trotting horses.

Herman Biddell, the Suffolk breed's greatest authority, described Blake's Farmer, foaled in 1760 and a famous Punch sire, as 'a trotting horse', chestnut in colour and 'not much above cob size' (about 15 h.h.). Writing about Mr Gleed's 'bung-tailed horse', foaled in 1805, he says, 'The horse himself gives the idea of a trotting cob. But he was a full-sized horse . . . '. These Roadster types or cobs – the Suffolk Cob was much the same as its neighbour over the border in Norfolk – were obviously lighter than the modern Punch but they were quite able to plough the light, sandy lands which form a part of the Orford hinterland.

Another earlier influence on the 'old breed', mentioned by Biddell, was Barber's Proctor, foaled in 1798. He was 'a trotting horse . . . the son of a racehorse . . . which appears to have been brother to a well-known racing stallion belonging to the Duke of Grafton, a grandson of Eclipse'.

The unique feature of the breed is that every living Suffolk traces its decent to a single stallion, Thomas Crisp's Horse of Ufford 404 (the Stud Book number), a horse foaled in 1768. Ufford is most probably a mistake, since the Crisps, owners of a stud of Suffolks, lived at Gedgrave Hall, *Orford* and there is no trace of a Crisp family at Ufford. Crisp's Horse travelled in the Woodbridge, Saxmundham and Framlingham area, which is still a natural centre for Suffolk breeding. He was described as being a short-legged, large-bodied bright 'chestnut' of 15.2 h.h. and as having a better head than most of his contemporaries. He was advertised as being 'able to get good

*A prize-winning Suffolk mare, Rowhedge Prudence, being run-out for the show judges.*

Above: *A pair of decorated Suffolks harnessed to an early omnibus is advertising that cannot be ignored.*

Below: *A team of Suffolks, bred to work the East Anglian soil, ploughing a Suffolk field.*

stock for coach or road' – a reflection of the background of traditional East Anglian trotting blood. Furthermore, all Suffolks are still 'chesnut', and the word is spelt that way. Seven shades of the colour are recognised by the Suffolk Horse Society that was formed in 1877 and they range from a pale, almost mealy, colour to a dark, almost brown, chesnut. The most usual is a bright, reddish colour and it, as well as the other shades, is the invariable product of the old sorrel or red roan.

If the modern breed owes its existence to one prepotent horse it owes much of its subsequent establishment to the authority already quoted, Herman Biddell of Playford. He was the Society's first secretary and devoted a lifetime to the breed, compiling over a period of nearly twenty years the first Stud Book. Published in 1880, it was entitled *The Suffolk Horse History and Stud Book* and was a wonderfully comprehensive work containing a history of the breed and of farming practice within the county, as well as a register of 1230 stallions and 1120 mares, lists of prize-winners from 1840 onwards and what still amounts to an excellent 'breed standard'.

The Suffolk was developed to meet specifically the conditions of its native county. It is a clean-legged horse, admirably suited to work the heavy clays of East Anglia but, also, because of its tremendous pulling power, it was much in demand for heavy work in the cities and towns.

A test which it seems was peculiar to the Suffolk fairs where Punches were offered for sale was to hitch the horse to a heavy, fallen tree for prospective buyers to assess his pulling strength. The tree did not necessarily have to be moved but the horse had to get right down on his knees before he was considered to have passed the test. This drawing attitude was to become typical of the breed, and the exceptional tractive power of the Suffolk is greatly assisted by the remarkably low shoulder, a conformational feature skilfully developed by the early breeders and ideally suited for heavy draught work. Another test was to ask the horse to rein back, an essential accomplishment for a draught horse working in city streets but unnecessary for a plough horse.

The modern Suffolk is a bigger horse than his forebears, standing around 16-16.3 h.h. but without there being any loss of depth through the girth. The measurement of the latter can be as much as 80 inches, which is greater than that of the Shire or Clydesdale.

The action is distinctive. The walk is sharp with a noticeable swing, whilst the trot, with only a modest degree of knee action, has a particular cadence not found in other heavy breeds. The writer Adrian Bell described it as 'a tense, slow trot as though to ease an overflow of strength'.

Because of the powerful chest there is considerable width between the forelegs which can sometimes result in a slight dishing action. The hindlegs, however, must be placed close together, though never 'cow-hocked', so as to allow the horse to walk a 9-inch furrow: 'If a horse had too much width between his hocks and is going between rows of sugar beet, he'll kick out more than he'll hoe.'

At one time the incidence of sidebone (a disabling ossification of the foot's lateral cartilages) in the Suffolk was a cause for concern and the feet were often less than satisfactory. This was corrected by the introduction, in the nineteenth century, of veterinary inspection of all animals in show classes and the modern Suffolk is notably sound in these respects.

Above all the Suffolk is an economical horse, maturing early and enjoying a long life span. His stamina and tractive power are unquestioned, but for all his strength and size he thrives on rations more modest than those needed to sustain other breeds. The routine of an East Anglian farm was for the horses to be fed at 4.30 a.m. Two hours later when the feed was digested they were led to work and with short rests continued through to 2.30 p.m. With other heavy breeds it was customary to stop work in mid-morning for the equine equivalent of 'elevenses' out of a nosebag, after which time had to be allowed for the feed's digestion.

Numerically, the breed is small, and declining numbers have caused concern in recent years. However, exports have been made to America, where there is a Suffolk breed society, and also to Pakistan where the Suffolk has adapted easily to the climate and has proved invaluable in the production of both army remounts and mules. Many of the European heavy horse breeds and a lot of the Russian ones also have benefited from infusions of Suffolk blood.

In Britain Suffolks are confined almost entirely to their native county where there are always classes for them at the shows. Woodbridge Show, early in the season, is regarded as the breed show.

Probably as great an ambassador for the Suffolk Punch as any of the East Anglian breeders and exhibitors is Roger Clark who with his wife Cheryl farms at Stoke-by-Nayland. Roger, one of Britain's most skilful and knowledgeable farriers and a Fellow of the Worshipful Company of Farriers, farms his arable land with a team of Suffolk Punches, using them for every sort of job from carting to ploughing. Cheryl, who is also a competent farrier, is just as capable as her husband at handling and driving the Suffolks and both enjoy their hunting, sharing the Mastership of the Essex and Suffolk Hunt.

*Hours of meticulous preparation are devoted to entries in the Clydesdale show classes.*

# 15

# *The Clydesdale*

Scotland's Clydesdale originates in the valley through which passes the River Clyde in the area we now know as Lanarkshire. It is not a breed of any great antiquity, having been developed over not much more than the past 150 years, but in terms of world influence it stands head and shoulders above all the other heavy breeds and has to be regarded, with the French Percheron perhaps, as the most successful.

Between 1715-20 the 6th Duke of Hamilton imported Flemish horses to improve the native draught stock and to increase their size. At the same time John Paterson of Lochlyoch imported horses of the same breed, probably from England, and founded a strain that was to become a major influence at least up to the mid-nineteenth century. Undoubtedly there were also infusions of Shire horse blood: indeed, it was probably a two-way traffic from which the Shire may have benefited as much as the Clydesdale.

Two noted nineteenth-century breeders were Lawrence Drew, steward to the 11th Duke of Hamilton at Merryton and his friend David Riddell. Both were dedicated to the improvement of the Clydesdale and both had scant respect for the Establishment – they actually set up the Select Clydesdale Horse Society in 1883 in opposition to the official Clydesdale Horse Society Stud Book which had been published five years previously. Very importantly, both were committed wholeheartedly to the introduction of Shire mares, firmly believing that Shires and Clydesdales were two wings of one breed. They were also connected with the two great nineteenth-century Clydesdale sires; Prince of Wales 673 and Darnley 222, whilst Riddell was one of the first exporters of the breed, creating a tradition of overseas selling which was to become the hallmark of subsequent Clydesdale breeders.

The success of Prince of Wales and Darnley, the former foaled in 1866 and the latter in 1872, was consolidated by the lines created by one stallion being put to the best daughters of the other. However, it is an earlier horse, Glancer 335, who is recognised as the breed's foundation stallion. He was the son of 'Lampit's mare', foaled in 1806, a mare who was held to be descended from the Lochlyoch strain, and his descendant was Broomfield Champion who appears in Darnley's pedigree and was the sire of Clyde (or Glancer 153) who through his sons left a particular mark on the breed.

The Clydesdale lacks the massive presence of the Shire and has none of the Suffolk's appealing rotundity, but of the three it is the best mover. It is described by the Society as having 'a flamboyant style, a flashy, spirited bearing and a high-stepping action that makes him a singularly elegant animal among draught horses'.

More importantly the Clydesdale is an essentially sound horse, generations of breeders having applied themselves assiduously to producing stock with good limbs and feet, breeding, indeed, for the 'wearing, enduring qualities of feet and legs'. Clydesdale judges will more often than not begin their examination of a horse by inspecting the feet. These are large, somewhat flat but very open with well-formed frogs, which suit the breed admirably for work on ungiving city streets, work in which the Clydesdale excels. On the other hand, they are less suitable for the plough horse, for they would be too big to fall conveniently in the furrow.

The modern Clydesdale is a lighter horse than those bred in the past and is now distinctive in type and appearance. The average height is around 16.2 h.h., although some may be larger, and the weight will be up to one tonne. The leg often appears long and will carry abundant silky feather. Joints, as in any horse, should be big, the hocks broad and clean and the knees flat. However, cow-hocks in the Clydesdale are a breed characteristic and are not considered to be a fault – 'sickle' hocks are, of course, another matter and are not acceptable. Clydesdale men want 'close' movement, with the forelegs being placed right under the shoulder and the hindlegs being placed close together. 'Cow-hocked' is the term applied when the hocks almost touch each other, the leg below the joint inclining outwards. The condition certainly reduces the speed potential and it is held that it causes uneven wear in the mechanism of the joint because the structure is out-of-true. 'Sickle hocks' are those which are noticeably overbent and curved inwards, like a sickle, on the front surface. They contribute to a marked loss of leverage.

Unlike the Shire, who sports a Roman nose, the Clydesdale has a straight profile and the neck is proportionally longer than that of the Shire. The shoulder, too, has more slope and the withers, higher than the croup in the interests of improved drawing power, are more sharply defined. The Clydesdale colour is predominantly bay or brown, but greys, roans and blacks are also found. White occurs on the face, the legs and underside of the body to an extent which would be unacceptable to Shire breeders but is common throughout the breed.

The preponderance of white markings together with the heavy feather which took time to clean and made the limbs susceptible to 'grease', an irritant, chapped condition of the heels leading to swelling and inflammation, was a disadvantage in most overseas markets but nonetheless the Clydesdale has been exported all over the world with great success. Clydesdales worked the great prairies of Canada and America, often in seven-horse teams to a three-furrow plough. They made a name for themselves in South Africa and New Zealand as well as in mainland Europe, and they earned the title of 'the breed that built Australia'. They will not be seen again on the prairie lands but they retain their popularity as forestry workers and in the cities of the world where 'the glamour of the Clyde turns an ordinary beer delivery into a public event . . . '.

Although the Clydesdale excites admiration, its record as a cross with British native ponies has rarely, if ever, been applauded and has even provoked harsh criticism of the breed. Certainly the Clydesdale blood did little good for the Highland, many Mainland specimens becoming heavy, lumpish animals as a result. It came near to being the ruination of the Dales Pony in the last century, and was condemned for its effect upon the Connemara. On the other hand Thoroughbred crosses have produced some remarkably good showjumpers, and three-quarter bred horses can be superb hunters and event horses despite some loss of speed. An extra infusion of Thoroughbred blood, to produce a seven-eighths bred horse, should, all else being equal, result in a very high-class cross-country prospect. Such crosses retain the activity and freedom of action of the Clydesdale and also possibly the rather large feet described euphemistically in the breed standard as being 'round and open', but which are just as often inclined to flatness. To offset the failings, however, there is the bonus of a wonderfully equable temperament.

*Decoration is a feature of the heavy show horse. A best decorated class is always held at the Royal Highland Show.*

Above: *Clydesdales were used at the 1984 Los Angeles Olympics to move the winners' podium in and out of the arena.*

Below: *This 18.2 h.h. Clydesdale colt was exported to Japan in 1990 from the Fairways Heavy Horse Centre, Perth, for the record sum of £20,000.*

# 16

# *The English Thoroughbred*

The Thoroughbred, the world's fastest, most valuable and most symmetrically proportioned horse, evolved in seventeenth- and eighteenth-century England largely as the result of the passionate enthusiasm of the English gentry and their kings for the sport of racing. Around this super-horse there has grown in the space of 250 years a vast, world-wide industry that generates immeasurable wealth. In that same period the Thoroughbred emerges as the greatest single factor in the formation of the world's modern horse population, its prepotent blood representing an essential element in the development of every sort of equine race outside the Arabian fountainhead.

The Thoroughbred's evolution is popularly attributed to three Eastern, or Oriental, horses which are regarded as the foundation sires. First, was the Byerley Turk, taken as a spoil of war by Captain Byerley at the capture of Buda from the Turks during 1686-87; then came the Darley Arabian, foaled in 1700 and acquired by Thomas Darley, the British Consul at Aleppo, in 1704 and sent by him to his family home at Aldby in East Yorkshire, where the Arabian died at the advanced age of thirty years. The third of the founding trio was the Godolphin Arabian, a fruitful source for numerous romantic legends. Foaled in 1724, he was brought to England by Edward Coke of Longford Hall, Derbyshire, four years later and was then acquired by Lord Godolphin.

Without doubt there is justification for regarding these three outstanding horses as the foundation of the Thoroughbred breed, but in reality, of course, the situation was far more complex. In the early days, when the definition of 'Thoroughbred' had yet to be made clear, there were a dozen or more other imported Oriental stallions that played important supporting roles. Nor should it be forgotten that it was only in England, with its long sporting tradition, that there existed an established base stock to provide the essential seed bed capable of producing a race of horses that would in a remarkably short compass become superior in terms of speed, power and mental vigour to any other, including its Eastern progenitors. In fact, there was already a pervading Eastern presence in the British equine scenario, a process which had begun when the Romans introduced Eastern blood to the native stock early in their occupation of Britain.

Long before the nations of the European mainland had developed a taste for racing, organised meetings and matches were integral to country life in England, particularly in the northern counties which were to play so large a part in the production of the Thoroughbred racehorse. Indeed, the Romans were staging races around the town of York probably as early as the third century AD, though the first recorded race-meeting took place at Smithfield, just outside the gates of London, in AD 1174.

Although regarded as the ogre of the British monarchy on account of the summary manner in which he rid himself of unwanted wives, Henry VIII, as well as being a considerable scholar and musician, was a devotee of the chase and of the sport of racing as well as operating a royal monopoly in the production of war-horses. All the three latter activities included the encouragement of horse-breeding. Henry, who was the first royal patron of racing, founded the Royal Paddocks at Hampton, importing horses from Spain and Italy which were certainly influenced by Eastern blood, most particularly by that of the North African Barb. These horses were crossed with the native 'running' stock already kept at the royal studs. Horses intended for racing were housed and trained at Greenwich under the direction of the King's Master of the Horse.

Henry's daughter, Elizabeth I, thrifty by nature and circumstance, continued the policy of interbreeding native stock with Spanish and Italian sires and founded another royal stud at Tutbury in Staffordshire. Her successor James I was even more concerned to promote the breeding of horses for hunting and racing, sports which he pursued with a rare dedication. James, however, moved continually towards the acquisition of more Eastern sires. He obtained the Markham Arabian, from the father of Gervase Markham (1568-1634), the equestrian authority of the seventeenth century and the author of numerous books and treatises. More horses were procured by him and shipped to England from the Middle East by Sir Thomas Edmond. It was James I who was responsible for putting Newmarket, the headquarters of British racing, on the map. He hunted there in the winter and built for himself a 'palace', or superior hunting lodge, and stables to house both his hunters and his racehorses. Records show that he was present at a race held on the

*The champion Thoroughbred stallion, Another Hoarwithy, at Newmarket 1990.*

Heath on 19 March 1619. His son, the ill-fated Charles I, continued the royal tradition, spending a lot of his time at Newmarket both hunting and racing. By 1625 regular spring and autumn meetings were being held and in 1639 a 'Gold Cup' was contested. Charles maintained studs at Eltham in Kent, Hampton Court and Malmesbury as well as the one founded by Elizabeth at Tutbury. All were large-scale enterprises, well-stocked and properly administered.

It seems reasonable, therefore, to suppose that the stock held at the Royal Studs up to the act of regicide in 1649, which deprived Charles I of his head and England of her monarchy, already contained elements of the continual and traditional Eastern infusions.

Following Charles I's execution, the Royal Studs were dispersed, Cromwell's Commonwealth regarding racing, along with dancing and, for a period, the Christmas festival itself, as frivolous pursuits and therefore sinful. At the time of dispersal Tutbury alone housed 140 horses. Interestingly, of the 38 mares included in the stud complement a number sported the word 'Morocco' in their names, a significant pointer to their *part* Eastern origin, for they were most probably half-bred out of English mares. Others included the name 'Newcastle' in their description. These would have been Spanish or Spanish/Barb crosses obtained by William Cavendish, Duke of Newcastle, the sole British master of classical horsemanship whose devotion to the Spanish horse was all-consuming.

With the accession of Charles II in 1660, the gentlemen of England were free to embrace the sport of racing once more with renewed enthusiasm, and attention now concentrated increasingly on the production of horses bred for sport – the criterion of Thoroughbred breeding to this day. The use of imported sires was accelerated, and the Eastern blood, whether it was called in the loose nomenclature of the age, Arab, Barb or Turk, assumed an even greater significance as the evolution of the horse we call Thoroughbred got under way. The practice of changing horses' names in accordance with changes of ownership was widespread, guaranteeing the greatest possible confusion among the historians of succeeding centuries.

Principal among the native 'running horses' with whom these sires were crossed were the swift Galloways of the north, the link between the ponies of the Highlands and those of the northern dales and fells, and the equally esteemed Irish Hobby. The modern Fell is deemed a descendant of the former whilst the Irish Hobby is the foundation of the Connemara pony.

Charles II developed Newmarket as the real centre of the Turf, involving himself closely with the formulation of races and the rules under which they were conducted. The situation of the town was ideally suited to the purpose: for the King it was close enough to

*Noblemen's horses in training on Newmarket Heath in the first half of the eighteenth century. Engraving by Peter Tillemans.*

London and to Parliament, and it was accessible to the breeders and trainers of the north, most of whom hailed from Yorkshire.

Sir John Fenwick, Master of the Horse to Charles II, acquired stallions from the Levant on the instructions of his royal master and he is also attributed with the import of the 'Royal Mares', a term which appears frequently in many early pedigrees. However, although that is the version appearing in the General Stud Book, it has been shown to be false. The mares were far more likely to have been supplied by James D'Arcy, Master of the Royal Stud, who also had a contract to supply the king with 'twelve extra-ordinary good colts' each year from his Sedbury stud, near Bedale in Yorkshire, for the not inconsiderable sum of £800 p.a. These mares would have been half-bred, that is from English stock by Eastern sires. Very few mares were imported in the century following the Stuart Restoration, the predominant influence on the evolving Thoroughbred being through the imported stallions, the most famous of whom were the accepted foundation sires.

The *Turf Register*, compiled by William Pick in the mid-eighteenth century, suggests that some 160 stallions might have been imported during the period: half appear to have been what we would call Arabian, the remaining fifty per cent being divided equally between Barbs and Turks, the latter possibly lacking the purity of lineage belonging to the Arab and inclining towards the Munaghi racing strain, like the horses of northern Iran.

It is a fallacy to assume that Eastern blood was used in the interest of increased speed. Neither the Byerley Turk, the Darley Arabian or the Godolphin ever raced, nor did any more than one or two of the imported sires, if the records are to be believed. The speed of the Arabs and Barbs was negligible and unimportant and on that account they were summarily dismissed by Gervase Markham. He held, from experience, that 'for swiftness' nothing exceeds the 'plane bredde' English horse and he gives numerous examples to support his assertion. Nevertheless he supported the use of the Arabian stallion unequivocally and after that, no more than a nose behind, the enduring Barb.

So why this continuous and exclusive use of Eastern blood to create a racehorse? The breeders of the seventeenth and eighteenth centuries, the men who created the Thoroughbred, should be recognised as being as expert as any before or, indeed, since. They, like their successors, needed to have the means whereby they could breed true to type if they were to accomplish their objectives successfully. The same applies to breeders of cattle, sheep or budgerigars.

The Arabs, the Barbs and the Turks had been bred very selectively in dry, relatively isolated, desert environments for centuries. They possessed as a result special qualities of refinement, hardiness and stamina, and they were prepotent to a degree. It was their prepotency – the ability to stamp their progeny indelibly with their characteristics – that the breeders tried to introduce into their own stock.

Nonetheless, despite the Arabian, which can be said to have founded and consolidated the breed, the Thoroughbred remains a hybrid derived from genetically diverse stock. Genetic uniformity has been achieved by centuries of selective breeding aimed at producing the characteristics applicable to racing performance. That uniformity makes the Thoroughbred influence predominant when combined with other breeds.

It has been established that 81 per cent of Thoroughbred genes today derive from 31 original ancestors of whom the most important are the three acknowledged founding stallions from whom all modern Thoroughbreds descend in the male line.

There was an additional stallion, the Curwen Bay Barb, who made an important gene contribution (5.6 per cent), but his male line failed to persist and that also applies to others: the Unknown Arabian, for instance, D'Arcy's Chestnut Arabian and D'Arcy's White Arabian, the Leedes Arabian, the Helmsley and Lister Turks as well as the

*A string of National Hunt racehorses exercising in the snor*

*nly in Britain and Ireland is steeplechasing a major sport.*

Brownlow Turk and Alcock's Arabian, the last two responsible for the grey colour character in the Thoroughbred.

The earliest of the three male line progenitors was the Byerley Turk, a horse who had more than his share of active service in the field. Having been captured at Buda he carried his master, then Colonel Byerley, at the Battle of the Boyne in 1690 before standing at Middridge Grange in Co. Durham and then at Goldsborough Hall, near York. He does not seem to have had many good mares but he was the sire of Jigg who established a male line that traces to horses like the Tetrarch and Tourbillon. His direct descendant was Herod, bred in 1758, whose progeny won over 1000 races. Herod is recognised as the first of the four tail-male lines, the others being Eclipse, Matchem and Highflyer, the latter Herod's son.

The Darley Arabian was shipped home as a four-year-old from Aleppo, Syria, where Thomas Darley was engaged as a merchant's agent and was also the British Consul. Of the three founding stallions the Darley would seem to have been the most striking in appearance and his pedigree was certainly more detailed than those of the other two. He was a bay horse of exquisite desert beauty with three white feet and a blaze who stood 15 h.h. and was splendidly proportioned.

*Eclipse by George Stubbs.*

Thomas Darley described him as being 'of the most esteemed race among the Arabs both by sire and dam, and the name of the race is called "Manicha"'. 'Manicha' is either a corruption of what hippologists now term Munaghi, or is it the other way about? Whatever the truth, it is the racing strain of Arab, a strain that whilst being much esteemed for its endurance and all-round ability does not always produce beautiful horses like the Darley.

Once more this horse did not cover a large number of mares but when mated with Betty Leedes he produced the first great racehorse, Flying Childers, described by his breeder Leonard Childers of Doncaster as 'the fleetest horse that ever ran at Newmarket, or, as generally believed, was ever bred in the world'. His full brother Bartlett's Childers did not race because of a propensity to break blood vessels, but he sired amongst others Squirt, the sire of Marske (he who was banished for a time to the anonymity of the New Forest), and Marske produced one of the greatest Thoroughbreds of all times, Eclipse, who was never beaten in his whole career and of whom it was said, 'Eclipse first, the rest nowhere'. From Eclipse descend today's important male lines of Blandford, Phalaris, Gainsborough, Son-in-Law, Boss, Teddy and St Simon. The Darley also heads the direct sire lines of Sun Chariot and Big Game.

The background of the third Arabian, the Godolphin, is less precisely documented and more subject to romantic legend. The most probable explanation is that this remarkable horse was of the Jilfan strain of the Yemen, was exported from there to Tunis via Syria and later given as a gift with three other Arabians to the King of France by the Bey of Tunis. Subsequently he was sold to Edward Coke, and then to Lord Godolphin.

The popular tale and the most far-fetched is that he was bought out of a Parisian water-cart and was then employed as the teaser to the stallion Hobgoblin at Lord Godolphin's Gog Magog stud. He is then reputed to have fought and defeated his superior to gain the favours of the mare Roxana, by whom – which is true – he got Lath and Cade. The latter sired Matchem, foaled in 1748, and so another influential line was formed which led to Hurry On and Precipitation. Matchem stood in the north of England and for most of his career commanded the then astronomical fee of fifty guineas. As a racehorse he was not as distinguished as his half-brother Gimcrack, who stood not much over 14 h.h. and is commemorated by the Gimcrack Stakes for two-year-olds held annually at York in August. But Gimcrack never came near to approaching Matchem as the leading sire of his day and one of continuing influence.

The all-pervading influence in the female line was that of Old Bald Peg, by the Unknown Arabian, who is the foundation mare of the

Thoroughbred breed. According to Lady Wentworth's table in *The Authentic Arabian* repeat crosses of this mare appear 367,162 times in the pedigree of Big Game; 233,579 in that of Sun Chariot; 138,827 in Hyperion, 113,740 in Fairway and 184,091 in the pedigree of Windsor Lad. Of the thirty-odd other tap-root mares in the General Stud Book to which all Thoroughbreds trace, there is a percentage of 'Royal Mares' and many more 'plane bredde' ones. The fact that most of the foundation mare stock of the late seventeenth and early eighteenth centuries were domiciled in the Vale of Bedale emphasises the northern influence in the evolution of the Thoroughbred.

After 1770 Arabs gradually ceased to be used in Thoroughbred breeding, better results being obtained with home-bred stallions and mares. Nonetheless, the Arab Stud Book remained within the General Stud Book up to 1965.

The Jockey Club, racing's ruling body, seems to have come into existence in 1752 when land was purchased in Newmarket on which the present Jockey Club building was erected. It was not until 1835, however, that a list of Jockey Club members was published, although the Club had exercised its authority since the mid-eighteenth century.

In 1791 the Jockey Club agents, Messrs. Weatherby, published *An Introduction to a General Stud Book* and Vol. 1 of the General Stud Book appeared in 1808. The word Thoroughbred, as applied to the racehorse, did not, in fact, appear until 1821 when Vol. II was published, and no official definition of the Thoroughbred was attempted right up to 1970. In that year in the Preface to Vol. 36 of the GSB (in which all genealogical records of racehorses in Britain and Ireland were included), it was stated that any horse seeking entry should be traceable at all points of its pedigree to strains already entered in previous volumes, those strains to be designated 'Thoroughbred'.

There are something upwards of 500,000 Thoroughbreds throughout the world today and in those countries where racing has become established its organisation is based on the British pattern.

In the early days of racing the emphasis was on distance races of up to four miles. Several heats might be run followed by a final, a matter which speaks volumes for the stamina and soundness of the early Thoroughbred. Far shorter races became the norm in the nineteenth century and that trend is reflected in the modern Classic races for three-year-olds.

The English Classics form the basis for those of other racing countries, although they may vary in distance from the English races. The five English Classics are: the St Leger (1¾ miles) run in September at Doncaster, where racing took place as long ago as 1595; the 1000 Guineas (for fillies only) and the 2000 Guineas, both run in

*Desert Orchid, the most charismatic jumper since Arkle, on his way
to winning the Arkle Challenge Trophy at Cheltenham.*

May over one mile at Newmarket; and the Derby and the Oaks (fillies only) run at Epsom in June over 1½ miles. The Triple Crown is a composite term given to the 2000 Guineas, the Derby and the St Leger. It was last won in 1970 by Nijinsky. There are 59 racecourses in Britain; 25 are given over to National Hunt racing; 16 to flat racing and 18 stage meetings under both rules.

Other countries have naturally developed their own Thoroughbred racehorses from the English base. The most influential racing nations, apart from Britain, are France, Italy and, of course, America which continues to be a dominant influence through sires like Bold Ruler, Secretariat and Seattle Slew, the last two being the winners of the American Triple Crown in 1973 and 1977 respectively.

The only countries, however, where the Thoroughbred horse is used extensively for the winter sport of steeplechasing are Britain and Ireland, both of which have very full jumping calendars from September through to April.

The most famous of the English races is the Grand National held at Aintree in March over four miles 856 yards and thirty imposing fences. It was first run in 1837 when it was won by The Duke, owned, it would appear jointly, by an inn-keeper, W. Sirdefield, and Mr Jonathan Williamson, a member of a prominent Lancashire family. The Duke was ridden by a well-known Cheshire horseman, Mr Henry Potts, a friend of Williamson. However, for all the undoubted glamour of the National, it is Cheltenham and particularly the Cheltenham Festival which is the Mecca of the steeplechasing sport and attracts the cream of English and Irish horses.

Britain and Ireland also have the amateur sport of point-to-pointing. These are races organised by almost every registered hunt in the country during the season from February to late April or early May. Originally they were races for hunters and were run literally from one point to another. Today, point-to-pointing is a more serious business. The horses are Thoroughbred and the races run over carefully constructed 'chasing fences on an oval course. The minimum length is three miles, and eighteen fences are an obligatory requirement. There are possibly a dozen or more point-to-point meetings held every weekend during the season.

The breeding of racehorses for the flat has often been called 'an inexact science' although breeders of flat race horses do enjoy certain advantages. Both sires and dams, for instance, have been tested on the racecourse and since they begin racing as two-year-olds their value as breeding stock is revealed at a relatively early age. This is not so with the 'chaser whose breeding is of necessity a far more inexact practice and something of a gamble to boot. Very few, if any, of the stallions used have ever demonstrated their ability to jump at speed and the

*Flying Childers by James Seymour.*

same applies to all but a minority of the mares. National Hunt racing is, indeed, the virtually exclusive preserve of the gelding. Few 'chasers are at their best until eight, nine, or even more, years of age, and so a successful sire of jumpers may not be recognised until he is past his prime or even dead. The breeder of competition horses faces the same difficulty in the selection of a stallion.

The sire of steeplechasers has to be picked, for the most part, on his flat race form, his conformation and his temperament. There have been entire horses who have won well over fences. Obviously they had jumping ability but they were not high-class racehorses and did not transmit the necessary exceptional qualities, particularly that of speed, to their offspring.

Ascetic emerged as the first top-class sire of 'chasers, siring three National winners between 1893-1906, but he was no good on the racecourse. His successor as a leading jump sire was Red Prince II who raced on the flat and over fences and after him came the little American horse, Battleship, who was 15.2 h.h. and won the Grand National in 1938. He lived until he was 31 and is recognised as a principal sire of jumpers. Another was Fortuna, winner of the 1947 Cheltenham Gold Cup, whose offspring, Fort Leney and Glencaraig

Lady, were both, like their sire, Gold Cup winners. In the 1960s and '70s Vulgan, a very good horse on the flat, was a memorable sire of jumpers and was followed by Deep Run, the Irish two-year-old champion in 1968.

Obviously, the uncertainties posed by the choice of stallion emphasise the importance of the mare's pedigree and there are, indeed, some notable female strains. Red Prince's dam, for instance, was the Grand National winner Empress whilst his sire was the flat racehorse Kendal. Bright Cherry, dam of the greatest 'chaser of modern times, Arkle, was herself the winner of six 'chases.

In eventing, Master Spiritus, sire of Ginny Leng's Master Craftsman, can be seen as a sire of particular note, along with Sam Barr's Welton stallions, founders of a whole line of consistently successful horses in the most demanding of equestrian sports.

Although sales of Thoroughbred horses, either youngstock or in training, are held at centres like Doncaster and Ascot, the principal ones are those held at Messrs. Tattersall's Park Paddocks at Newmarket. The firm was founded by Richard Tattersall who left Yorkshire in 1745 to purchase an interest in Beevor's Horse Repository in London and to become manager of the Duke of Kingston's stud. Later he leased land and premises at Hyde Park Corner where the Jockey Club met and where Tattersall staged twice-weekly horse sales.

Tattersall, a shrewd businessman, combined his sales with his own breeding enterprise. He sold his young stock rather than keeping them to race and so became the first commercial breeder of the Thoroughbred. His stock was in great demand largely because of his acquisition in 1779 of Highflyer, the son of Herod, who is recognised as the founder of one of the tail-male lines of the Thoroughbred.

Tattersall's son, Edmund, moved the business to Knightsbridge Green in 1865 and a variety of stock was sold there up to the Second World War. After the war the sales were moved entirely to Newmarket, where Tattersalls had conducted purely Thoroughbred auctions on a fairly regular basis since the end of the eighteenth century. Today, the famous rotunda with its statue of a fox, which had been a feature of the Knightsbridge sale complex, dominates the much larger Park Paddocks where some seven hundred horses can be accommodated. The first mixed sale is held in April and is followed by similar ones in July and September. In October there are the yearling sales and then the prestigious Houghton Sales, Europe's most important yearling sale. After the Houghton there are the Autumn Sales and finally, the mammoth week-long December Sales which attract buyers from all over the world.

Although Thoroughbred blood has been used consistently to up-

Above: *Flat racing, 'the sport of kings', at Kempton Park, the popular track close to* London. Below: *Tattersalls – auctioneers of top-class Thoroughbreds.*

grade the majority of modern horse breeds and is, indeed, the one essential element in the production of competition horses for the ridden disciplines and often for carriage driving, too, its widespread rise in these fields is incidental to the breed's main purpose. Specifically, the Thoroughbred is produced to race at top speed on carefully prepared, level surfaces. For that purpose conformation, temperament and soundness are not really considerations nor are they of very much importance in comparison with the overriding criterion of speed. So long as a stallion or mare is likely to transmit speed to their progeny that is a good enough reason for them to be put to breeding.

Nonetheless, extensive use is made of the Thoroughbred outside racing, and so long as it is used in conjunction with stock that is constitutionally sound and so on the desirable characteristics of the Thoroughbred will be retained in some degree in the subsequent progeny. There will, for instance, be an increase in speed and athletic ability and, most importantly, in mental stamina and the all-important quality of courage. Not for nothing is it said that 'an ounce of blood is worth a pound of bone'.

In Britain the use of selected Thoroughbreds to produce hunters and competition stock is encouraged by the National Light Horse Breeding Society (HIS) which began its life as the Hunters' Improvement and National Light Horse Breeding Society and still retains the HIS as a postscript to its title.

The HIS (as the Society is still generally known) was initially an offshoot of the important Hackney Horse Society, but in 1885 it became a society in its own right and its object as it was stated in that year by Wyndham B. Portman, founder and proprietor of *Horse and Hound*, the world's leading equestrian weekly, was 'that of encouraging by all means the use of sound, suitable sires for the propagation of hunters . . . ' and he went on to deplore the use of 'unsound, travelling wretches . . . sowing worthless brutes broadcast throughout the land'.

To that end a Premium Stallion Scheme was instituted in 1888 and it remains central to the Society's activities today. Some fifty-odd premiums are awarded each year in March at the Society's stallion show held at the Newmarket Park Paddocks. These premiums, each of £500, together with fourteen super-premiums ranging from £1500 to £1025 for the horse in fourteenth position, are made possible by the grant made by the Horse Race Betting Levy Board. They allow the owners of half-bred mares to take advantage of the services of sound, healthy Thoroughbred stallions at a fee that would otherwise be out of the reach of the small breeder. All the Premium stallions are inspected for soundness and suitability and are certified as being free from hereditary diseases.

The HIS also operates a Graded Mare Register and one for Half-bred Stallions (i.e. Cleveland Bays, Irish Draughts, Welsh Cobs etc.). The National Hunter Show, the proof of the pudding as it were, is held annually at Malvern in early September and the sales of stock by Premium stallions are held each year at Bridgwater, Harrogate and Malvern.

The total production of the Premium Stallion Scheme does not exceed two thousand foals a year, which is far smaller than that of Germany or France, for instance. Nonetheless, the record of HIS horses is remarkable in relation to the number bred and it cannot be approached by any other country in Europe. Twenty years ago horses by HIS stallions were winning an average of seven hundred races a year and that has been maintained to this day. Many of these are point-to-point winners, but a good percentage win professional races and at least one, Aldaniti, was a winner of the Grand National. This horse, ridden by Bob Champion, won in 1981 and was by Derek H, a horse who was a consistent Premium winner at Newmarket.

Eventing in Britain is largely dominated by the progeny of HIS stallions and a fair percentage of the Badminton field is usually sired by Premium horses. The winner in 1991 was The Irishman, sired by a particularly successful HIS horse, Good Apple, half-brother to Snow Knight, winner of the 1974 Derby.

Many more Premium-bred horses provide good, sound horses for many hundreds of people to go hunting on and, perhaps, to exhibit at county show level and to compete locally in jumping, horse trials and dressage competitions.

In general, the pure Thoroughbred is not suited temperamentally to dressage. Of course, there are exceptions, but the confines of the arena and the degree of submission demanded are often too restrictive for a horse of his highly-strung nature and courage. Nor is the Thoroughbred ideal for showjumping and that is not just because of his temperament. His conformation is conducive to speed and whilst he is well able to jump fast over wide, spread-type fences, like those encountered on the racecourse, his length of stride, low action, and the long proportions of the hind leg are not ideal for jumping the big, upright obstacles which will be included in the top national and international courses.

Nonetheless, no competition horse can be expected to perform effectively without carrying a considerable percentage of Thoroughbred blood, a fact amply recognised by warm-blood breeders, whose product, already based on heavy Thoroughbred infusions, has to be reinforced continually from this reinvigorating source.

*A Thoroughbred stallion being led at exercise at the Aston Upthorne Stud, Berkshire.*

### THE ANGLO-ARAB

An obvious offshoot of the Thoroughbred is the cross with the pure-bred Arab, from which the former in part originated.

In France, intensive use is made of the Anglo-Arab, a horse which has been carefully developed and which outnumbers the pure-bred. The French Anglo-Arab is a well-proportioned, tough, athletic horse with a long record as an above-average performer in all sorts of sports. It shares the Stud Book with the pure-bred and for inclusion must have a minimum of 25 per cent Arab blood. In the well-organised and generously funded French system with its network of national studs it is officially recognised as an 'improver' and plays a significant role in the breeding of the *Selle Français*, which is probably as good a warm-blood as any in Europe.

In Britain, the Anglo-Arab is a cross between a Thoroughbred horse and an Arab mare, or vice versa, with their subsequent re-crossings and has its section in the Arab Horse Society's Stud Book. There have been some very good Anglo-Arabs in Britain even if they do not compare with the French product. However, their number and their influence in British breeding generally is not significant and their potential goes unrecognised largely because the breed is not encouraged or promoted sufficiently.

Possibly as great a handicap as any to the breeding of what should be a supreme example of the riding horse is the unfortunate reputation enjoyed by the pure-bred Arab in Britain. Although in recent years Arab racing under Jockey Club rules has become established as a popular sport for breed enthusiasts and Arab horses have largely dominated the sport of long-distance riding, few breeders of competition or even general-purpose riding horses have much good to say about the Arab. Some Arabs can jump, although in that respect they are limited by their size and conformation. Very few, however, are as bold about leaving the ground as the average half-bred hunter or native pony and they are certainly not as versatile.

To the hunting fraternity the Arab is an anathema and to much of the riding public the AHS is seen as a society outside the mainstream of British equestrianism and the Arab as an in-hand horse for the fancier with little relevance to the modern riding requirement.

To what extent that is really true is probably arguable but whilst that image persists the Anglo-Arab is unlikely to feature as one of the success stories of British breeding.

# 17

# *The Hackney*

Although racing was the 'sport of kings' long before Charles II made Newmarket its headquarters, there was in 'Old' England a powerful parallel tradition of trotting horses that typified the most robust facets of the English character.

In the laws and proclamations of the Middle Ages, as well as in numerous commentaries, mention is made of 'trotting' horses as opposed to the fashionable ambling horses – that is those trained to a slow pacing gait, which were much employed by persons of rank as a comfortable mode of travel. The latter, however, were not suited to the purposes of war, hence Henry VIII's Statute of 1542 which required the nobility, as well as anybody wealthy enough to wear a silk gown or have his wife turn out in 'any French hood or bonnet of velvet' to keep a specified number of 'stoned trotting horses', (i.e. entire horses – stallions).

That 'breed' – and Henry's ordinances recognised the trotting horse as such – was even then esteemed and well established in Norfolk. As the Norfolk Trotter it survived to become the all-round travel horse of the eighteenth and nineteenth centuries with the ability to carry a heavy man at speeds of up to 16-17 m.p.h. and to do so over distances and on ground that often afforded far from perfect going underfoot. Galloping on the racecourse or in the hunting field was all very well, but for practical travelling the trot was the pace on which to depend. Up to the early nineteenth century these formidable Trotters, just as frequently called Roadsters, were used under saddle by the able-bodied as the most expeditious means of travel where there were no established roadways, and they were much preferred to journeying by the heavy, ill-sprung coaches of the day which were hauled painfully over rough and rutted tracks. Naturally enough, sporting Englishmen took great pride in the prowess of their Trotters, and matches, resulting in some remarkable records, were commonplace among men who did not regard riding sixty miles or more in a day as being anything out of the ordinary. In time, as the roads improved, the emphasis shifted to the harness horse, but just as frequently the Trotters continued to excel in both roles.

Their present-day descendants are the spirited Hackneys of the show-ring, distinguished by the brilliance of their spectacular high-stepping action. Up to and after the First World War it was they and their carriage-horse companions who dominated the show classes in a way that is not exceeded today even by the modern showjumping competitions. Today's Hackney is certainly a less substantial animal than his leg-at-each-corner Norfolk forebear, and his greater refinement, as well as the necessarily restricted use that can be made of him, can give the impression of artificiality. Nonetheless, he retains all the fire, courage and soundness of constitution which characterised his trotting ancestors.

The Hackney's role today as a pure show horse reflects inevitably the impossibility of the breed ever being driven again on the open roads of the twentieth century, except in a few strictly controlled situations. It serves also, perhaps, to obscure the Hackney's place in English history and the significant contribution of the breed to every sort of European carriage horse, as well as to some of the continental mainland's saddle breeds. Nor are these fields the sole extent of the Hackney's influence, for it also extends into the American breeds, in particular to the world's supreme harness racer, the Standardbred.

The development of the Thoroughbred racehorse in the seventeenth and eighteenth centuries ran parallel for a time to that of the trotting Roadster, and both originated from the *same source* of Eastern blood. The difference in the subsequent development of these two most singular breeds lies in the social structures from which they emanated. The Thoroughbred, of outstanding and continuing importance, was the result of the absorbing interest of the landed classes in racing and hunting. The Trotters, from whence came the Hackney, were utilitarian horses developed very largely by practical horsemen of the agricultural community to serve their particular requirements. That it satisfied their sporting instincts as well was coincidental, however much they relished the opportunity to test one good horse against another. The Jockey Club from its beginnings had had its full aristocratic complement, but the first council of the Hackney Stud Book Society, founded in 1883, included fifteen farmer-breeders, two auctioneers, three horse-dealers, a few landowners and three wealthy fanciers. Half a century later, when horse-breeding had become almost uneconomical, farmers on the council had been replaced by tradesmen, seven of whom were butchers who would have employed Hackneys in the conduct of their

*Hackney show harness, clearly showing the over-check used to position the head.*

businesses, whilst the horse-dealers had also risen to seven.

All modern Hackneys trace their descent from the horse which has become generally known as the Original Shales, a horse which Henry F. Euron, first secretary of the Hackney Horse Society and the indefatigable historian of the breed, described as the 'fastest horse' of his day and the first noteworthy 'Hackney stallion'. Euron established, after disproving a previous attribution, that Original Shales was a son of Blaze out of a 'Norfolk' mare. Blaze, foaled in 1733, was the son of the great Flying Childers, and was therefore the grandson of the Darley Arabian. It is this horse, of authenticated pedigree and of unmistakable desert type, that is at the root of the Norfolk Roadster and also of its compatriot the possibly less well-known but equally important Yorkshire Roadster.

Original Shales's most notable sons were Driver and Scott Shales. The latter's son, Thistleton Shales, was the sire of Marshland Shales, possibly the most famous of all the Shales family and a horse who epitomised everything that men desired of the Norfolk Roadster. A chestnut, Marshland Shales was barely 15 h.h. He was not, we learn from *The Sporting Magazine* of April 1824, 'a remarkably high goer though he bent his knees well'. He was then owned by Messrs. Hawes of Coltishall, Norfolk, and the same source tells us that he had an 'immense' crest which fell over to the off-side in his later years. The horse was never beaten in all the numerous trials he contested 'and was universally acknowledged both the speediest and the stoutest trotter of the time . . . He was fully master of 20 stone (280 lbs) and most truly, as they used to style in Norfolk, "a thundering trotter".'

The feat which made Marshland Shales's reputation was when in August 1810, as an eight-year-old, he trotted seventeen miles in 56 minutes on the Kings Lynn road against Richard West's Driver, whom he beat easily by about one-and-a-half miles. He was then owned by John Chamberlain of Magdalen and at the last minute was ridden by Mr Osbert Spinks, the lad engaged to ride having been 'got at'. Spinks was a sixty-year-old farmer with an interest in the horse and weighed 12 stone (168 lbs), whilst Driver's rider rode at three stone less than that.

The admiration, amounting to reverence, extended to the great trotting horses of the period has never been better captured than in George Borrow's *Lavengro* (1851) when he described the entry of Marshland Shales to the fair at Castle Hill, Norwich, and records that the crowd became silent and men took off their hats in respect for the old, one-eyed horse.

'Amain,' wrote Borrow, 'I did for the horse what I would neither do for earl or baron, doffed my hat; yes! I doffed my hat to the wondrous horse, the fast trotter, the best in mother England; and I,

*Marshland Shales. From a painting by E. Cooper of Beccles, engraved for the* Farmer's Magazine *1823.*

too, drew a deep "Ah!" and repeated the words of the old fellows around: "Such a horse as this shall never see again, a pity that he is so old.'"

There were, of course, other splendid lines cast in the same mould, many of them capable, as they claimed for Marshland Shales, of trotting up to twenty miles an hour. The Fireaways of Lincolnshire were notable and made a lasting impression on the breed. One of the Fireaways went to Yorkshire to make a mark for himself in that county, his name being changed to Kirby's Wildfire. An even greater influence in the north, however, was the Norfolk Phenomenon, bought by Robert Ramsdale and his son Philip of Market Weighton.

Although Norfolk and Yorkshire trotters shared a common ancestry there was for some years a difference in type. The Norfolk horses were often sturdy and cob-like whilst the Yorkshire sort were lighter and had a shade more quality. Today, of course, in the modern Hackney these regional variations have been eliminated, the best characteristics having been fused into an elegant, showy harness horse of between 15-15.3 h.h. with a unique action that is described as being 'effortless in the extreme', 'electrical and snappy at its zenith' and giving 'the impression of a mystic, indescribably deliberate, instantaneous poise'. In part the modern, extravagant, action, which would have found no favour in the days of the early Roadster, can be taught and improved by skilful training, but at its root it is largely inherited from generations of trotting horses bred selectively on pedigree, performance records and the strength of their physical attributes.

The American Standardbred, the finest harness racer in the world and a pacer because of the influence of early Spanish horses in America, has its origin in the Thoroughbred of the eighteenth century, the early foundation of the breed being through Messenger, who raced on the flat in England and went to America in 1788 to spend twenty years at stud. By Mambrino he had a line to Blaze and also to Sampson, a horse who did trot. Messenger's overwhelming influence comes through his closely in-bred descendant Hambletonian 10 (Rysdyk's Hambletonian), foundation sire of the modern Standardbred. Foaled in 1849 Hambletonian sired 1335 offspring between 1851-75. This raw-boned, rather plain horse reinforced his trotting background by being out of a Charles Kent mare by the Norfolk Trotter Jary's Bellfounder.

The most important Norfolk-bred stallion in modern Hackney history is D'Oyley's Confidence 158, virtually a pure-bred Norfolk Trotter with four crosses to Bellfounder and seven to Marshland Shales. He sired the champion stallion of the first Society show at Agricultural Hall, Islington, in March 1885. This was William Flanders's Reality, Norfolk-bred from a dam by the Thoroughbred Tamworth. William Burdett-Coutts, founder of the very influential Brookfield Stud in 1887 and a founder member of the Hackney Stud Book Society, expressed some revealing reservations about D'Oyley's Confidence although he wrote that 'I would readily give £10,000 to buy him and keep him in this country.'

Burdett-Coutts, who was an astute judge, expressed the opinion that there was 'a strain of softness and a strain of cartiness somewhere in the blood of the old horse [Confidence], both of which come out in his stock bred from Hackney mares'. He considered that the failing could best be countered 'by an infusion of Thoroughbred blood', as in the case of Reality, or by using the horse and his sons on 'the harder basis of the Yorkshire Hackney'. The interesting point is the acceptance of Thoroughbred blood as an up-grading influence. There was already, as we have seen, a strong Thoroughbred connection to the Yorkshire horses and it is the later infusions which gave the Hackney its spirited character and an additional brilliance of movement. Two of the most famous of the Yorkshire Hackneys were Denmark 177 (1862) and Lord Derby II 417 (1871). They, with Confidence and Fireaway 249 (1859) and Wildfire 1224 (1880), the last two both Yorkshire bred, are considered to be founding fathers of the modern Hackney.

Above: *Ingfield Black Prince, Hackney Horse of the Year at the 1990 Wembley Show, demonstrates the breed's brilliance* of action. Below: *The Hackney Pony, sharing the Stud Book with the horses, retains the same superlative movement.*

The best Norfolk and Yorkshire horses of the latter part of the nineteenth century were eagerly sought after by continental countries and a great many were exported – to the long-term detriment of British breeding. Indeed, Yorkshire can claim credit for having founded a famous Hungarian breed with a horse from one of its most renowned studs, that of the Cooks on the Yorkshire Wolds at Huggate and later at Thixendale. It was Cook's Wildfire who sired a horse called North Star in 1854. He was sold to Colonel Frederick Barlow of Woodbridge in Suffolk and in 1860 the Colonel sold him to the Austro-Hungarian Government. North Star, a horse who himself carried a substantial percentage of Thoroughbred blood, stood at the great Hungarian stud of Mezohegyes and with the English Thoroughbred Furioso sired a good half-bred breed called Furioso-North Star, from the base stock of Nonius mares.

The Hackney Pony (under 14 h.h.) shares the Stud Book with the larger Hackney Horse. It has all the brilliance of the Hackney action as well as the fire and courage, but it is a real pony with pony character.

In essence it was the creation of one man, Christopher Wilson of Kirkby Lonsdale in Cumbria. By the 1880s Wilson had created a distinctive stamp based on the local Fell Pony with some help from the Welsh Ponies of North Wales. He had, for example, a pony called Little Wonder whose sire was the Norfolk foundation horse, D'Oyley's Confidence 158 and the dam a Welsh mare. The breakthrough came with the use of the pony stallion Sir George, a winner of eight Royal Agricultural Society first prizes. He was by Sportsman, a Yorkshire horse tracing his descent from the archetypal Norfolk Phenomenon in a direct line to Flying Childers. The female progeny by Sir George from Wilson's selected mares were in time put back to their sire and, wrote Sir Walter Gilbey, 'threw foals which showed elegant and true Hackney characteristics in far more marked degree than did their dams . . .'.

Walter Gilbey, twice President of the Hackney Horse Society, was the owner of the Elsenham Stud, where he bred horses and ponies of many breeds. He is accounted as one of the greatest authorities of the past century and had an important influence on the overall development of British breeding.

These 'Wilson ponies', as they were long known, lived out and were left to forage for themselves on the fells during the winter, a practice which not only kept the height down to the limit required but also preserved the hardiness of constitution.

At the turn of the century wealthy men like Gilbey and Burdett-Coutts were establishing large breeding studs and well into the 1920s there was a thriving and lucrative export trade in Hackney Horses and Ponies. The American-born Burdett-Coutts, who was Member of Parliament for Westminster up to his death in 1921, did much to encourage exports to his native country and some very big studs were set up with his help in the Eastern states and the Middle West.

Without doubt, however, the dominant world influence in the breeding and exhibiting of both Hackney Horses and Ponies since the First World War were the Blacks, Bob and James, and then Bob's daughter Cynthia and her husband Frank Haydon. Between the wars the Blacks were the most successful Hackney men in Britain or, indeed, elsewhere, and the Haydons carried on the tradition with their almost unbeatable Hurstwood horses and ponies.

Cynthia Haydon exhibited Hackneys in single and pair harness from an early age and was unsurpassed in the show-rings of both Britain and America. She was taught to drive a team by the late Bertram Mills, of the great circus family, and she drove his team at Olympia, London, before World War 2. Cynthia Haydon was the first woman ever to compete in the International Driving Three-Day Event in both European and World Championships and the first to drive a team of Hackneys in this highly competitive sport. Her reputation, up to her recent retirement from active competition, was as great in America and Canada as it was in Britain and she drove regularly in New York and at Toronto's Royal Winter Fair.

The early Trotters, as we have seen, were saddle horses and so were many of the horses referred to in the records of the Hackney Stud Book Society when that body was formed for the purpose of 'the publication of a Stud Book for Hackneys, Roadsters, Cobs and Ponies' – the objective and the number of types to which it refers is worth noting. Significantly, in view of the Norfolk connection, the first registered office of the Society was at the premises occupied in Norwich by the *Norwich Mercury* newspaper.

Most of the trotting records made early in the nineteenth century were performed under saddle, but it is not generally realised that Hackneys were shown under saddle up to the late 1930s, particularly in the North of England, where they were usually entered in the harness classes as well, and up to 1929 there were also ridden classes at the New York National Horse Show. As late as the mid 1960s an attempt was made to revive ridden Hackney classes at some British shows but 'the time was out of joint' and the need for a high-actioned riding horse had for long been irrelevant in the modern horse scene.

These ridden Hackneys were usually shown in a long-cheeked curb bit, the riders sitting well back in the flat saddle for all the world like the American Saddlebred classes which they so much resembled. Indeed, before the Saddlebred became so popular Hackneys and part-bred Hackneys were frequently shown in classes for three-gaited horses, that is those shown at walk, trot and canter.

The Hackney could very easily be equated with the Saddlebred, to which it is distantly related. Both are generally regarded as being 'artificial' products and the training methods employed in each respect will occasionally attract criticism. Possibly on that account little consideration is given to the Hackney as a potential element in the modern competition horse.

Some Hackney breeders did attempt to preserve what they termed 'the old riding type'. Lord Ashtown's stud at Woodlawn, Co. Cork, in Ireland, for instance, bred Hackney riding horses up to about 1941 and the Monson family of Walpole St Peter, near Wisbech in Cambridgeshire, had an old strain that produced predominantly grey hunters. This stud was also closed during the Second World War.

Hackneys and Hackney/Thoroughbred crosses used to have a reputation for being good jumpers and there is no reason at all why they should not be equally successful in that sphere today. They have courage, an athletic quality and a hindleg and hock joint ideally suited for jumping. The high hock action and the ability to bring the joints well under the body allows for an enormous upward thrust calculated to take horse and rider over the biggest upright fence. As jumpers it was the American-bred Hackneys that achieved the most success. The Toronto dealers, Crow and Murray, specialised in such horses. One of their most famous jumpers was Confidence, a pure-bred Hackney who stood 16.1 h.h. He won at the International Horse Show at Olympia in 1910 and in the same year cleared 7 feet 2 inches to win a class at the New York National. Later, at Syracuse, ridden by the Harvey Smith of the day, Dick Donnelly, he jumped 8 feet 1½ inches. There are not many present-day showjumpers capable of clearing that height.

Another Crow and Murray horse, Sir Ashton, was just as big a winner at the National and, when his name had been changed to Greatheart, he jumped a record 8 feet 2 inches at Chicago under Fred Vesey.

One of the most remarkable Hackney jumpers was the 13.2 h.h. Bathgate Swell, originally produced as a harness pony. He won at the 1910 New York National and in the following year was ridden by Colonel P.A. Kenna VC of the 21st Lancers at Olympia, where he was second in a class of 106 for the Connaught Cup.

Between the wars, indeed, the showjumping scene was full of Hackneys and Hackney part-breds. Tosca, one of the winning German team at the 1936 Berlin Olympics, was one of them. Tommy Glencross, the British artist of the jumping sport in the 1930s, used Hackney crosses and so did the Machin-Goodalls. Vivian, later Mrs. George Boon, who rode Neptune at Badminton on more than one occasion, had Why Not? when she rode as a junior and then horses like Hoodoo and King's Rhapsody, all Hackney crosses. Oorskiet, a notable South African-bred horse of the Sixties, was another successful Hackney cross.

Hackneys could still have a role to play in the production of a British competition horse but it seems unlikely that there will be much movement in that direction in the foreseeable future. As James Agate, that most articulate *aficionado* of the breed, wrote, 'Harness horse exhibitors live in a curious little world of their own, they take a wholly professional and expert interest in harness classes, and in little else at horse shows.'

Another notable horseman, R.S. Summerhays, the doyen of the horse world for over half a century, was as keen a driving man as he was a rider, but in the 1930s he was describing the Hackney men as 'a funny crowd' and they are, indeed, still an element apart from the general equestrian scene in Britain and are regarded by followers of other disciplines in that light. Those wishing to test the truth of those assertions can view the 'curious little world' of the Hackney fancier at the annual breed show which is held in June in conjunction with the South of England Show at Ardingly, Sussex.

The name Hackney with a capital H was adopted by the breed Society on its formation in 1883, the capital letter marking the difference between the high-stepping carriage and show ring horse, bred and schooled to display an extravagant action, and the breed's less specialised predecessors, the active riding horses of general utility. These latter were known universally as hackneys and more often than not they might amble like the palfrey, which was the same thing under a different name. The Society became the Hackney Horse Society in 1891 when the office moved to London.

The term derives from the French *haquenée*, in Old French *haque*, and the Spanish equivalent is *haca*, meaning a nag or gelding. It was brought into use in England by the Normans and it distinguished the light riding horses and amblers from the larger war-horses. The roll of horses killed at the Battle of Falkirk against the Scots in 1298, which was prepared for the assessment of compensation, included a number of 'hackneys'.

Rather later, when it was commonplace for saddle-horses, or hackneys, to be let out for hire, those who ran such businesses became known as 'hackney men' and so hackney began also to refer to a hired horse. Thereafter the word was extended, in one of those illogical quirks of misuse, to cover a carriage let out for hire and we have hackney coaches and hackney cabs. Even now a taxi may be granted a 'hackney' licence – which is a far cry from an ambling saddle-horse of the Middle Ages or, indeed, from the modern show horse.

Above: *A team of Hackneys driven to a coach by Mrs. F. Haydon, one of the foremost whips of the post-war era.*

Below: *Hackney classes are a prominent and popular feature of the major British horse shows.*

# 18

# *British Horse and Pony Types*

Lacking the support of state-financed studs and an integrated breeding system Britain has, nonetheless, contrived to produce a number of distinctive equine types whose equal is not found elsewhere.

## THE RIDING PONY

The Riding Pony, in terms of proportion and quality is the most nearly perfect equine in the world, particularly when it is in the 13.2 h.h. division. Its evolution was made possible by a handful of extraordinarily prescient and dedicated breeders who employed a judicious mix of the Arab, Thoroughbred and native breeds to produce their ideal pony type. The native base was provided by the Welsh ponies and to a lesser degree by the elegant Dartmoor, itself owing something to infusions of Welsh blood.

Confirming the compatibility of Eastern horse stock with the indigenous pony is the amalgam of blood producing the dynasty of Riding Ponies based on the Arab, Naseel, and the foundation mare Gipsy Gold. This mare was out of Tiger Lily, a Welsh Mountain Pony, by a small polo-type Thoroughbred, Good Luck. Mated with Naseel (Raftan out of Naxina) she produced a line of Riding Ponies, the best known of which was the legendary Pretty Polly. Pretty Polly was the undisputed champion of the early 1950s and she bred no less than nine champions, among them Pollyanna and Polly's Gem.

Pollyanna went to America, where she swept the board in American performance classes, whilst Polly's Gem, like her dam, also produced a number of notable champions. Her greatest achievement was Gem's Signet, a quite remarkable pony, who was the result of her mating to Bwlch Hill Wind. Indeed, that mating united the two great Riding Pony lines, for Bwlch Hill Wind, by Bwlch Zephyr, was the grandson of the legendary Bwlch Valentino, the stallion who played the greatest part in the establishment of a virtually fixed type Riding Pony – that is, a pony of Thoroughbred form, proportion and movement that still retains all of the pony characteristics.

Valentino owed his quality and brilliant action to a polo pony stallion sire, the little Thoroughbred horses which have exerted enormous influence on most of the pony breeds. His sire, registered in the Argentine Stud Book, was Valentine, by Malice, by Malandante and Malice's grand-dam was an Arab mare. Valentine's dam was Bwlch Goldflake and she was by Meteoric out of Cigarette, a part-bred Arab whose dam was a Thoroughbred/Welsh cross – and so the essential trinity of bloods is once more apparent. Cigarette was the prolific winner of flapping races throughout Wales for ponies under 13.2 h.h. Flapping races, i.e. races not held under Jockey Club rules, were commonplace in Wales up to very recent years and played a part in the evolution of riding ponies of all sorts based on Welsh blood.

The influence of these stallions and their sons, like Oakley Bubbling Spring, Valentine's son out of Bubbles, who was by the Arab, Count Dorsaz, was inestimable and resulted in an acceptable and unmistakable type of Riding Pony that is quite unique and represents a breeding achievement approaching the 'invention' of the Thoroughbred horse itself.

The criticism levelled against the Riding Pony is that it is too sharp, too highly-couraged for a child, and that by approaching the Thoroughbred in proportions and constitution it lacks the bone, substance, hardiness and temperament which should all be essential attributes in the child's pony. On the whole these are fallacious arguments, often advanced by ardent but less than knowledgeable admirers of the native 'hairies'. The latter, of course, cannot be expected to compete against the brilliantly moving show pony which in action, conformation and presence dominates the show pony classes in all divisions – 12.2 h.h., 13.2 h.h., and up to 14.2 h.h.

From the pure Riding Pony has evolved the Working Hunter Pony which performs in the ring over a jumping course. The classes are divided according to the pony's height and the child's age and the emphasis is on jumping ability. Then there is the Hunter Show Pony which, in perfection, is a miniature middleweight hunter. Both are essentially practical mounts for young people and have obvious uses outside the show-ring.

## THE HUNTER

By definition a hunter is a horse capable of hunting and that applies to a legion of variously conformed animals that take to the field during

Above: *The British Riding Pony, possibly the most elegant and perfectly proportioned of all the equines.* Right: *A supreme example of the hunter, the champion King's Warrior by the HIS Premium stallion Good Apple.*

the hunting season between November and April. Specifically the term defines a horse that is up to carrying a rider expeditiously and safely for perhaps two days a week, and doing so without suffering any unsoundness which would prevent his regular participation in the sport. In essence hunting calls for a tough, bold customer, constitutionally hard, having the stamina to gallop and jump in a good, average country. Obviously, types vary from one hunting country to another. In the English Shires a near-Thoroughbred horse is needed if one is to keep in touch with hounds. In more enclosed countries, in plough or in the hills, a powerful, short-legged sort, half- or three-quarter bred perhaps, that will jump tricky places may be more suitable. Whatever the country, however, a horse of good conformation and, therefore, good balance is needed and he must be inherently sound as well as being temperamentally suited to the job.

Beyond any doubt the best cross-country horses are bred in Ireland and Britain, where the sport of hunting has its origins. The good hunter is often half- or three-quarter bred, that is he has either 50 or 75 per cent Thoroughbred blood, or it could be more. In general the greater the percentage the greater will be the speed and scope. The best base for the breeding of hunters is usually regarded as being the Irish Draught, but obviously there are other possible crosses with the Thoroughbred; Clevelands, for instance, and the heavy horse breeds. As good as any and very much better than most are those crosses which include a background of native pony blood, Connemaras, New Forests, Dartmoors, Welsh breeds and the rest, excluding obviously the little Shetland. They introduce soundness, pony sagacity, stamina and sheer ability to the subsequent progeny.

Many, if not most, of the Thoroughbred sires used for hunter breeding in Britain are the stallions made available under the Premium Stallion Scheme operated by the National Light Horse Breeding Society (Hunter's Improvement Society) described in the chapter on the Thoroughbred horse.

In the English show-ring, show hunters, which are not required to jump, are judged on conformation, the action at walk, trot, canter and gallop and on the ride they give the judge. To these requirements may be added the quality of 'presence', which may be defined as personality so immediately arresting as to demand attention. Only in Britain and Ireland do judges ride exhibits and in no other countries are horses assessed in this manner.

Show hunter classes are divided into weight divisions: lightweights able to carry up to 12 stone 7 lbs (175 lbs); middleweights to carry between 12 stone 7 lbs and 14 stone (196 lbs), and heavyweights able to carry over that weight. There are also classes for small hunters standing between 14.2 h.h. and 15.2 h.h. and for working hunters (lightweights up to 13 stone 7 lbs (189 lbs) and heavyweights) who are expected to jump a course of fences, the greater percentage of marks being given for performance.

## THE COB

A peculiarly appealing and very English or Irish type is the cob, who is more likely to be the result of chance breeding than otherwise, although many have Irish Draught, heavy horse or Welsh Cob blood in their parentage mixed with a dash of Thoroughbred.

A show cob in Britain has a height limit of 15.1 h.h. but cobs can be found up to about 15.3 h.h. The declared advantage of the smaller animal is that the decrease in height allows the animal to be more easily mounted by the older and less agile. In essence, indeed, the cob, a short-legged, strong-bodied 'stuffy' (compact) sort of horse, should be a suitable mount for an elderly rider who has put on a little weight and requires a steady, unflappable ride that can still gallop and jump. In fact the cob, capable of carrying 14 stone (196 lbs) and upwards, is a gentleman's gentleman and is usually a considerable character as well. He is, indeed, a John Bull horse that was once used for both riding and driving and is not found other than in the British Isles where he is regarded with a particular affection.

In days happily gone by cobs were docked, a cruel practice which is now illegal. Today, their tails are carried full but their manes are hogged giving them a sporty, jaunty and knowing look.

## THE POLO PONY

Polo ponies, and whatever their height they are still called 'ponies', have been bred in Britain and Ireland ever since the game was introduced to this country in the nineteenth century by British soldiers and civilians who had learnt it in India. Britain's National Pony Society was founded in 1893 and was originally the Polo and Riding Society, much concerned with the encouragement of polo pony breeding. Indeed, polo sires, basically small Thoroughbreds with perhaps a native pony cross, were much used in the upgrading of the pony breeds.

The recognised polo pony foundation sire, appearing in the Society's first Polo Pony Stud Book was Sir Humphrey de Trafford's Rosewater, a Thoroughbred. The height limit then in force was 14 h.h. and to preserve the size native ponies were admitted to the Polo Pony Stud Book Vol. V in 1898-99. The height limit was abolished in 1916 and 'ponies' may now be of any height, most of them averaging around 15 h.h. or an inch or two more. A prime example in the

Left: *A champion show hunter with presence, exemplary conformation and with galloping ability.*

Right: *A gentleman's gentleman, full of character, up to weight and well able to gallop and jump.*

Below: *Grandstand, one of the greatest cobs of recent years, is a pure-bred Irish Draught.*

evolution of the modern New Forest Pony, for instance, is the polo stallion Field Marshal who stood in the Forest just after the First World War when the height limit had been abolished. He was by a Thoroughbred sire out of a Welsh mare.

The result of the abolition of the height limit was that it left a number of small stallions out of employment, as it were. They provided, however, the Thoroughbred element in flapping ponies and ultimately in the Riding Pony, and in some instances were beneficial influences in the development of native stock.

Polo started in America in 1878 at the instigation of the newspaper tycoon James Gordon Bennett Jnr., after a visit he had paid to Hurlingham, the headquarters of British polo, two years previously.

The game was first played in the Argentine about the same time by British residents there and by the 1930s the Argentine, closely followed by America, had become the world's leading polo nation. The game became a way of life on the huge ranches of the pampas and the Argentine-bred ponies were soon recognised as the best in the world, a position they hold to this day.

The Argentine pony is a particular and recognisable type. It is fast, tough, very agile and wiry. Its speed and quality come from the Thoroughbred, its toughness of constitution from the native Criollo base which was continually upgraded by infusions of Thoroughbred blood. Many Argentine ponies are today imported to Britain and, of course, the mares – as most of them are – will be bred from when their playing days are over.

## THE HACK

The word hack, like Hackney, derives from the Norman French word *haquenée* which referred to a light saddle-horse. The concept of the hack, however, is entirely British, although show-ring classes for hacks are held on the same pattern in countries as far off as New Zealand, Australia and South Africa. Today, the hack in Britain is a specialised animal produced for the show-ring, which it graces with a unique elegance.

However, it was not always so. Before the advent of the horse-box and trailer, hunters were taken on quietly to the meet by their grooms, whilst their owners followed on a '*covert* hack' cutting a dash at a comfortable, but fast enough 'hack canter'. The *covert* hack was usually a Thoroughbred riding horse, elegant, well-schooled, and attractive and showy enough to set off its owner to best advantage. It was a horse lighter in build than the hunter, and since it did not have to carry weight through a full hunting day it did not need the latter's bone and substance.

Even more refined, however, was the beautiful '*park* hack', brimful of presence and so beautifully schooled that it could be ridden on the fingers of one hand. It was a horse on which a well-tailored gentleman might show off his clothes and his good taste in female companions as he escorted a lady in London's Rotten Row under the appraising and often critical public eye. The hack was required to move in all its paces with lightness, great gaiety, freedom and perfect balance.

Today's show-ring hacks are predominantly Thoroughbred and incline far more to the *park* hack than to the heavier *covert* hack whose type is more likely to be seen in the classes for 'riding horses'. But whatever the hack's breeding it is expected to be a *horse* and to show no pony characteristics.

Like its predecessor the park hack, the show-ring horse is expected to be well-schooled and well-mannered, and to be infinitely light and graceful. It must not, however, be a 'blood weed' and, indeed, it should be a model of conformation with not less than 8 inches of bone below the knee. Hacks are shown at the three gaits of walk, trot and canter. They are not required to gallop but each entry must give an individual show on which much depends. In accordance with the British convention the horses are also ridden by the judge.

British show classes are for small hacks (14.2-15.2 h.h.); large hacks (15-15.3 h.h.) and ladies' hacks (14.2-15.3 h.h.), the latter being ridden side-saddle.

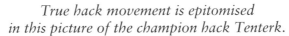

*True hack movement is epitomised*
*in this picture of the champion hack Tenterk.*

173

Above: Polo, *the game played at 40 m.p.h. with the ball travelling 60 m.p.h. faster than that.*

Right: *A good stamp of Argentine polo pony. A very fast and agile pony capable of playing high-goal matches.*

Left: *An elegant, very well-made show hack. A Thoroughbred whose manners match the very correct conformation.*

# Breed Societies

Arab Horse Society
Windsor House, The Square,
Ramsbury, Wiltshire SN8 2PE

British Show Pony Society
124 Green End Road, Sawtry,
Huntingdon, Cambridgeshire

Cleveland Bay Horse Society
York Livestock Centre, Murton,
York YO1 3UF

Clydesdale Horse Society
24 Beresford Terrace, Ayr, Ayrshire
KA7 2EG

English Connemara Pony Society
2 The Leys, Salford, Chipping Norton,
Oxfordshire OX7 5FD

Connemara Pony Breeders Society –
Ireland
73 Dalysfort Road, Salthill, Galway

Dales Pony Society
196 Springvale Road, Walkley,
Sheffield S6 3NU

Dartmoor Pony Society
Whitethorne Cottage, Hittisleigh,
Exeter EX6 6LG

Exmoor Pony Society
Glen Fern, Waddicombe, Dulverton,
Somerset TA22 9RY

Fell Pony Society
Greylands Cottage, Larriston Farm,
Newcastleton, Roxburgh TD9 0SL

Hackney Horse Society
Clump Cottage, Chitterne,
Warminster, Wiltshire BA12 0II

Highland Pony Society
Beechwood, Elie, Fife KY9 1DH

Irish Draught Horse Society (GB)
4th Street, National Agricultural
Centre, Stoneleigh,
Warwickshire CV8 2LG

National Light Horse Breeding Society
(HIS)
96 High Street, Edenbridge,
Kent TN8 5AR

New Forest Pony and Cattle Breeding
Society
Beacon Cottage, Burley, Ringwood,
Hampshire BH24 4EW

Shetland Pony Stud Book Society
Pedigree House, 6 Kings Place,
Perth PH2 8AD

Shire Horse Society
East of England Show Ground,
Peterborough, Cambridgeshire
PE2 0XE

Thoroughbred Breeders Association
Stanstead House, The Avenue,
Newmarket, Suffolk CB8 9AA

Welsh Pony and Cob Society
6 Chalybeate Street, Aberystwyth,
Dyfed SY23 1HS